Learning Chinese The Easy Way

The first book of Chinese characters

Sam Song

For information about books to be published,
please visit
        http://www.discoverchinese.cn/
Or contact the author at:
        samsong.author@msa.hinet.net

Publicity

To request the author for an interview or
for an appearance at an event (conference,
speaking engagement, etc.), please email
samsong.author@msa.hinet.net

Acknowledgements

Special thanks and love to John Paul, Carol Creed,
Frederick Reeves, Jordan Smith, Matt Flint,
Kathy Christensen, George FERRANTE,
Anthony BIANCARDI, Craig Zaidel,
Christian BOGUE, Melissa KAWA,
DeAnna Walton, Mrs. Lockett,
Soniz RUIZ, Juanita Moreland,
Shane and Tammy Carpenter,
Jean Strauss, S. W. SONG,
Lindsey Lou Lichfield,
J. SONG, J. Chen

SS

Introduction

After remembering the story, it will be very helpful and easier to remember all the characters in the story!

~ **CONTENTS** ~

The Wind and The Sun 风与太阳(風與太陽)

Introduction

Chinese character

Every Chinese thinks that each Chinese character is a word because it represents a complete concept just like each English word does, while most English speakers refer to it as a Chinese Character. For the purposes of keeping things simple and avoiding any confusion, this book use the term "Chinese character."

Writing Chinese characters

In the first several years of Chinese students' schooling, kids do learn to write new characters because it's helpful to remember new characters. The writing process is also the important and necessary coordination training for children's finger muscles to make the writing more beautiful day by day. For beginners, while reading the book, it's recommended to draw or write each new character at least several times.

Chinese character and stoke order

Learning to write Chinese characters by hand is one of the ways to gain a thorough understanding of each character. Chinese characters consist of strokes that are "usually" written in a specific order.

The most important rule to follow when writing strokes is: Horizontal strokes are written from left to right and vertical strokes are written from top to bottom.

 This shows an outline character, 走, shown in the book.
The numbers illustrate the sequence of the strokes.

Every stroke has two ends and as a general rule the location of the number on or around the stroke shows which end the stroke starts. For example, ⤴, 5 is on the left side of the stroke, so the stroke is written from left to right.

The following diagram shows how to write the character stroke by stroke.

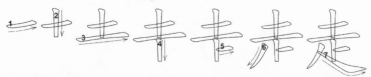

Introduction

Traditional and Simplified characters

The Traditional Chinese characters have existed for a long time in China, and some Chinese characters have been simplified by common usage.

In an attempt to increase literacy, starting in the 1950s, the government of China decided to include some Traditional characters in the official written language, and it has even made some new Simplified characters available, although many Traditional characters were left untouched in that process. (**Also it's essential to point out that the spoken language, Mandarin, remains the same**.) As a result, **the written Chinese characters used in China are called "Simplified Chinese characters" or "Simplified Chinese."** Generally speaking, Simplified Chinese characters are currently used worldwide, though many people outside of China still use what is called "Traditional Chinese characters," or "Traditional Chinese."

Please note, for the most commonly used Chinese characters, Simplified Chinese keeps more than 70% of the Traditional Chinese characters.

Pinyin – Chinese pronunciation

Pinyin is the Romanized system used to represent the pronunciation of Chinese characters. Pinyin uses the same alphabets as English, though Pinyin also uses the extra letter 'ü' and four tone marks. Pinyin is very useful for those who are learning Chinese and is used in China and throughout the world.

In this book, next to new Chinese characters, you may notice Roman characters. Below is an example:

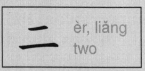

"èr" or "liǎng" is the Pinyin, or pronunciation, of the Chinese character, 二, which means "two" in Chinese.

At the end of each story, there is a Pronunciation Reference, with Mandarin phonetic symbols, for all Chinese characters from the book.

Introduction

Download audio files

www.discoverChinese.cn
samsong.author@msa.hinet.net

Please download audio files at the author site above. So, while reading the book, you can listen to the pronunciation of Chinese, character by character, phrase by phrase, sentence by sentence, and finally the complete story.

Story approach to learn Chinese

Contextual learning is very important and one of the best ways to learn Chinese characters. This book takes a story approach to introduce Chinese characters.

This book is the level 1 book, which contains the following 2 stories in both Traditional Chinese and Simplified Chinese:

Two Men and The Bear 二人與熊 二人与熊
The Wind and The Sun 風與太陽 风与太阳

The book, **Learning Chinese The Easy Way Level 1: The Fox and The Goat (New)** ISBN: 1467918695 published Nov. 2011, contains the third story in both Traditional Chinese and Simplified Chinese:

The Fox and The Goat 狐狸與山羊 狐狸与山羊

(The book, **Adventures in Mandarin Chinese The Fox and The Goat** ISBN: 1439218129 published Nov. 2008 (9 reviews), is a stand-along book though it also contains the third story in both Traditional Chinese and Simplified Chinese.)

Workbooks for the above books:
Tracing & Writing Characters and Sentences (Simplified Characters) ISBN: 1466449136
Learning Chinese The Easy Way L1 Workbook (Traditional Characters) ISBN: 1475015348

Learning Chinese The Easy Way Level 2 (ISBN: 1466336994 or 1475009372) contains 700 Chinese sentences, 330 Chinese characters, 3 Chinese songs, and a most popular dialogue.

Learning Chinese The Easy Way Level 3 is scheduled to be publsihed in 2012.

Chinese Character Practice Sheet (Example)

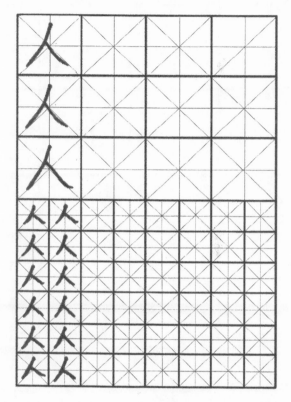

The above shows a handwritten representation of the Chinese character that means "person". Please use the boxes to write this character the best you can. You will find it helpful to continue writing out new characters at least three times when you come across them in this book.

Chinese Character Practice Sheet (Sample)

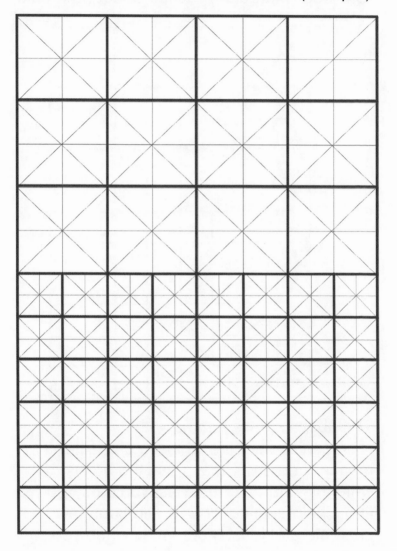

Learning Chinese The Easy Way
(Traditional & Simplified Characters)

Story 1
Two Men and The Bear

二 人 与 熊
二 人 與 熊

 **Unveil**

the foundation of

Chinese characters!

*After studying through this story,
you will be able to read
the famous fable
" Two Men and The Bear"
in Chinese to your children,
students, friends, and colleagues!
They will be amazed!*

二 èr, liǎng
two

Have you ever thought about how easy some Chinese characters could be?

It is easy to learn that **one** is 一, **two** is 二, and **three** is 三 in Chinese.

For a long time, the Chinese have adopted and used the Arabic numbers, such as 1, 2, and 3 as Chinese numbers. Also, when used as a number, 一 and 1, 二 and 2, 三 and 3 are often used interchangeably in Chinese by the general public.

There is no difference in 一, 二, and 三 between Traditional Chinese and Simplified Chinese.

English	one	two	three
Chinese	一	二	三
	1	2	3

The characters, 三三二二 sān sān liǎng liǎng, can be used to mean "(people come in) in twos and threes."

From this point on in this book, I will mention the Simplified Chinese character only if it is different from the Traditional Chinese character. In most cases, they are identical.

TC: Traditional Chinese   SC: Simplified Chinese

TC	SC	Pinyin	TC	SC	Pinyin
一		yī, yí, yì	二		èr, liǎng
三		sān			

* As a general rule, 一 is pronounced yī as an ordinary number, but when 一 precedes a fourth tone Chinese character, 一 is pronounced yí, otherwise, 一 is pronounced yì or yī.

(Beginners sometimes speak Mandarin using the wrong tones. Even so, they usually still can be understood by most Chinese as long as they speak Mandarin at a slower speed.)

** Generally, "2" is pronounced èr, though "2" also can be pronounced liǎng when "2" is followed by a measure word, which is a Chinese character, such as 隻 or 只 on page 9, that denotes the form or shape of an item.

You have learned:

一 二 三

人 rén
person; people

How do we construct a character that means "person" in Chinese?

If we see a person at a distance, it may look like , or 人. In Chinese, 人 rén means "person" or "people."

Generally, Chinese grammar is simpler than English grammar. As a general rule, all Chinese nouns, such as 人, do not change at all between their singular and plural forms. 人 rén is an example - there is no difference between "person" or "people" for 人. Below are all correct in Chinese:

one person yī rén	two people liǎng rén / èr rén	three people sān rén
一人	二人	三人
1 人	2 人	3 人

You have learned (Simplified Chinese):
二人
liǎng rén   Two people

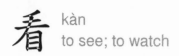 kàn
to see; to watch

How do we construct a character that means "to watch" in Chinese?

 This photo shows a young girl is watching something outdoors. She used one **hand** (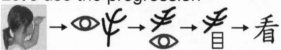) to keep the sunlight out of our **eye**s (👁). This scene conveys the concept, **to watch**.

Let's use the progression

👁✍ → 看 → 看 → 看

to reach the character, 看 kàn, that means "to see" or "to watch" in Chinese.

👁 This is a sketch of a beautiful eye. Let's use the progression

👁 → ⊕ → 目 → 目

to reach the character, 目 mù, that means "eye."

You have learned (Simplified Chinese):
二人看
liǎng rén kàn　Two people saw

到 dào
to arrive

How do we construct a Chinese character that means "to arrive"?

 This drawing looks like "a *person* is watching a *bird* swooping downwards to seize something on the *ground*."

土 ——Lots of plants growing from the earth
——The surface of the earth
——Earth

The above picture shows the Chinese character, 土 tǔ, that means "soil," "earth," or "dirt." We can use 土 to signify "ground."

Let's use the progression

ground 土 → 刂 → 至 刂 → 到

to reach the character, 到 dào, that means "to arrive." 至 looks like a bird approaching the ground as it catches its prey. 至 zhì means "to arrive" in Chinese.

You have learned (Simplified Chinese):

二人看到
liǎng rén kàn dào   Two people saw

熊 xióng
bear

How do we construct a character that means "bear" in Chinese?

 This drawing shows two bears and a bear footprint.

Let's use the progression

to reach the character, 熊 xióng, that means "bear" in Chinese. The drawing, ⱴⱴ, is used to signify "a bear footprint in the wild."

Because a bear can be very energetic, the character, 能 néng, is used to mean "energy" in Chinese. Some extended meanings of 能 are "to be capable of," "can," "energy," or "ability."

You have learned (Simplified Chinese):

二人看到　熊
liǎng rén kàn dào　xióng
Two people saw　bear

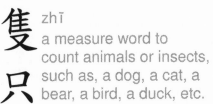

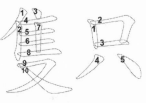

zhī
a measure word to
count animals or insects,
such as, a dog, a cat, a
bear, a bird, a duck, etc.

How do we construct a character to count animals in Chinese?

This drawing shows the sketch of a bird.

This is a sketch of a bird with a short tail.

业, 义, or 父 This is a sketch of a hand.
Let's use the progression

父 → 业 → 又 or 又

to reach the character, 又, which can be used to signify a hand.

This drawing shows a bird captured by a hand.

Let's use the progression

隻 → 隻 → 隻 → 隻 → 又 → 只

to reach the character, 隻 zhī (1st tone), that is used as a measure word, in Traditional Chinese, to count animals or insects, such as, a dog, a cat, a bear, a bird, a duck, etc.

隻 is 只 in Simplified Chinese.

English	One bear	Two bears	Three bears
Pinyin	yì zhī xióng	liǎng zhī xióng	sān zhī xióng
TC	一隻熊	二隻熊	三隻熊
	1 隻熊	2 隻熊	3 隻熊
SC	一只熊	二只熊	三只熊
	1 只熊	2 只熊	3 只熊
SC(TC)	一只熊(一隻熊)	二只熊(二隻熊)	三只熊(三隻熊)

TC: Traditional Chinese   SC: Simplified Chinese

The character, 只 zhǐ (3rd tone), is used to mean "only" in Chinese.

You have learned (Simplified characters):
二人看到一只熊，   liǎng rén kàn dào yī zhī xióng，
Two people saw a Bear.

Have you noticed that Chinese verbs don't change as the tense changes? Each Chinese verb, such as the above character 看, has only one form, which remains the same in any tense. (Since obviously this is an old story, we used the simple past tense (saw) in English.)

立刻 lì kè
Immediately

How do we construct characters that mean "immediately" in Chinese?

 This drawing illustrates a person standing on the ground.

Let's use the progression

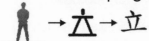

to reach the character, 立 lì, that is used to mean "to stand" in Chinese. 立 also conveys the concept, "ready to act."

This picture shows a person is coughing.

Let's use the progression

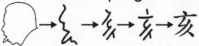

to reach the symbol, 亥, that can be used to signify "a cough." A cough is a sudden expulsion of air from the chest.

This drawing shows the sketch of a butcher's knife.

Let's use the progression

㇆ 囗 → 刀 → ノ 丁 → 丿人 → 丿丨 → 刂

to reach the character 刀 and 刂.

刀 dāo means "knife" in Chinese.
The character 刂 is a radical for "knife." It means that 刂 can be used as a component of a character, such as the character, 刻.

* dāo *is onomatopoeia. We may hear the* dāo *sound while chopping a knife biting the chopping block.*

By putting 亥 and 刂 together, 刻 kē (1st tone) is used to mean "to engrave" in Chinese.

* *The engraving sound,* kè, *is similar to the sound of a person coughing; and, like a cough, each engraving sound is very short usually.*

Also ancient Chinese used knives to engrave records of the time passed. They divided a day into 100 parts. Each part was written as, 刻 kè (4th tone), and it stands for "15 minutes," or, "a very short period of time" in Chinese.

In conclusion, 立 conveys the concept, "ready to act" and 刻 can mean "a very short period of time." 立刻 lì kè means "immediately."

You have learned (Simplified characters):
二人看到一只熊，一人立刻
... yī rén lì kè ... One person immediately

爬 pá
to climb

How do we construct a character that means "to climb" in Chinese?

 This drawing shows the sketch of a crawling lizard.

Let's use the progression

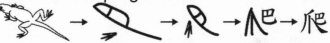

to reach the symbol, 爬 pá, that conveys the concept, "crawl," "to crawl," or "to climb." 巴 bā conveys the concept, "to stick to." 爪 zhuǎ means "claw."

You have learned (Simplified characters):
二人看到一只熊，一人立刻爬

liǎng rén kàn dào yī zhī xióng，yī rén lì kè pá

Two people saw a Bear. One person immediately climbed

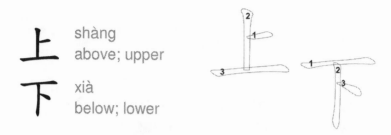

上 shàng
above; upper

下 xià
below; lower

How do we construct a character that means "above" in Chinese?

⸚ This was used to signify "above" in ancient China several thousand years ago. Later, people also used this symbol, ⸚ or ⊥, to signify "above." Over time, the symbol, ⊥, was mixed with ⸚, creating 上 shàng, which means "above" or "upper."

Originally, people used the symbol (⊤, ⊤, or ⊤) to show something that's "under" another object. Over time, the symbol, ⊤, was mixed with ⸗, creating 下 xià, which means "below" or "lower."

You have learned (Simplified characters):
二人看到一只熊，一人立刻爬上
liǎng rén kàn dào yī zhī xióng，yī rén lì kè pá shàng
Two people saw a Bear. One person immediately climbed into

樹 树 shù tree

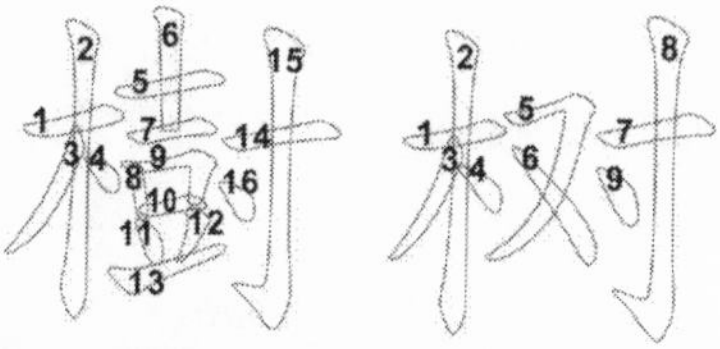

How do we construct a character that means "tree" in Chinese? Let's look at a sketch of a tree first!

 This drawing shows a brief sketch of a tree, while the symbol, , signifies branches growing upwards and the symbol, , signifies "roots."

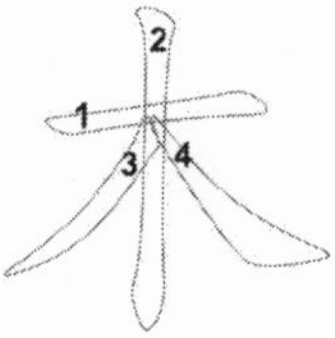

Let's use the progression

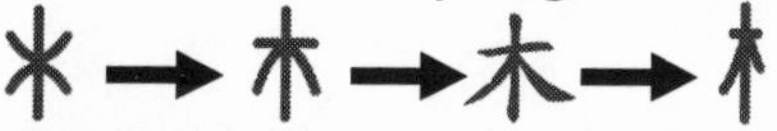

to reach the character, 木 mù, which means "wood."

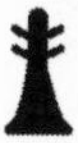 This drawing shows the sketch of a tree.

Let's use the progression

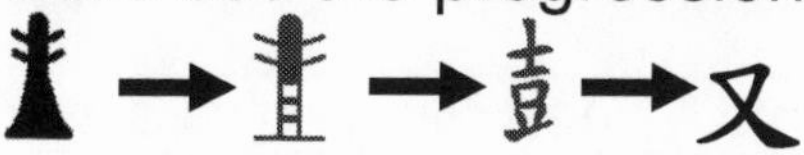

to reach the symbol, 壴, that can be used to signify a tree.

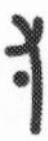 This drawing looks like "a hand 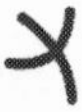 picking

fruits from a tree."
Let's use the progression

彐 ➝ 寸

to reach the symbol, 寸, which can be used to signify "a hand picking fruits from a tree."

By putting 木, 壴,, and 寸 together, 樹, contains three main features of a tree. The character, 樹 shù, is used to mean "tree" in Traditional Chinese. The character, 木, is used as the radical for "wood" or "tree." Putting 木, 又, and 寸 together, 树 shù means "tree" in Simplified Chinese.

一只熊爬上树。(一隻熊爬上樹。)
yī zhī xióng pá shàng shù   A bear climbed into a tree.

You have learned (Simplified characters):
二人看到一只熊，一人立刻爬上树，
liǎng rén kàn dào yī zhī xióng，yī rén lì kè pá shàng shù，   ... One person immediately climbed into a tree.

climb a tree	climb into a tree	climb down a tree
爬树	爬上树	爬下树
pá shù	pá shàng shù	pá xià shù
A person climbs a tree.	A person climbs into a tree	A person climbs down a tree
人爬树	人爬上树	人爬下树
rén pá shù	rén pá shàng shù	rén pá xià shù

另 líng another 力 lì strength

How do we construct a character that means "another" in Chinese?

⼑ This drawing shows the sketch of a plow, which can be used to signify "strength." Let's use the progression: ⼑ → ⼒ → 力 to reach the character, 力 lì, that means "strength" in Chinese.

The character, 口 kǒu, means "mouth" or "entrance" in Chinese.

This picture illustrates that "**another** person is using a plow." We can use 口 to signify a "person" here, because everyone has a mouth. Putting 口 on the top of 力, the character, 另 líng, signifies "another one." So, the character, 另 means "another."

另一人 líng yì rén means "another person."

You have learned (Simplified Chinese): 二人看到一只熊，一人立刻爬上树，另一人

馬 上
马 上

mǎ shàng
immediately

How do we construct two characters that mean "immediately" in Chinese? Let's look at a horse sketch first!

This drawing shows a brief sketch of a horse.

, , or This drawing shows the head of a horse and the bridle to control the horse by the rider.

•••• This drawing can be used to signify "a horse's feet running very fast."

Let's use the progression

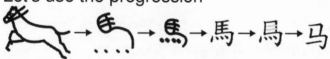

to reach the character, 马(馬) mǎ, that means "horse." The word, 马上(馬上), signifies "sitting on a horse and being ready to act," so 马上(馬上) mǎ shàng means "immediately."

Both 立刻 and 马上(馬上)(literally "a person already on a horseback (ready to go and do a job)") mean "immediately" in Chinese. Many Chinese don't pay attention to the difference between 立刻 and 马上(馬上), so, often 立刻 and 马上(馬上) are used interchangeably by most Chinese.

立马(立馬) lì mǎ still means "immediately" in Chinese. (立马(立馬) is short for 立刻马上(立刻馬上).)

As stated earlier, the character, 上, means "above" or "upper." 上 also means "to get on."

to get on	to mount a horse	to dismount a horse	immediately
上	上马(上馬)	下马(下馬)	马上(馬上)
shàng	shàng mǎ	xià mǎ	mǎ shàng

You have learned (Simplified Chinese):

二人看到一只熊，一人立刻爬上树，另一人马上

liǎng rén kàn dào yī zhī xióng，yī rén lì kè pá shàng shù，lìng yī rén mǎ shàng

Two people saw a Bear. One person immediately climbed into a tree. The other person immediately

倒 dǎo
to fall over

How do we construct a character that means "to fall over" in Chinese? Let's look at the Chinese character 倒 directly.

If we break apart the character 倒, it contains 3 parts: 亻, 至, and 刂.
If we see a person at a distance,

it may look like 大, 𠆢, 人, 卜, or 亻,

The character, 亻, is used as a radical for "person."

When we learned the character, 到, earlier, we also learned the character, 至 zhì, which means "to arrive."

As we learned earlier, the character 刂 is a radical for "knife."

By putting 亻, 至, and 刂 together, the character, 倒, can be used to signify "a knife reaches a person" or "a person gets killed or hurt." So, the character, 倒 dǎo (3rd tone), means "to fall over."

As stated earlier, 下 means "below" or "lower" in Chinese. So, by putting 倒 and 下 together, this 下 makes the meaning of 倒下 more complete and 倒下 dǎo xià means "to fall over." However, in this story, 倒下 means "to purposely fall down - (to play dead)."

You have learned (Simplified Chinese):

二人看到一只熊，一人立刻爬上树，另一人马上倒下

liǎng rén kàn dào yī zhī xióng，yī rén lì kè pá shàng shù，lìng yī rén mǎ shàng dǎo xià

Two people saw a Bear. One person immediately climbed into a tree. The other person quickly and purposely fell over down upon the ground.

死 sǐ
dead; to die

How do we construct a character that means "dead" in Chinese?

This drawing shows a dagger.
Let's use the progression

to reach the character, 匕 bǐ, that is used to mean "dagger."

This drawing signifies the sketch of a hanging head that is bleeding.

Let's use the progression

Ȱ → 歺 → 歹

to reach the symbol, 歹, that signifies "a hanging head that is bleeding." The character, 歹 dǎi, means "evil" or "bad."

Putting 歹 and 匕 together, the character, 死 sǐ, is used to mean "dead" or "to die" in Chinese.

You have learned (Simplified Chinese):
二人看到一只熊，一人立刻爬上树，另一人马
上倒下　死

装装 zhuāng
to pretend

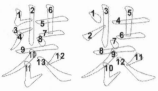

How do we construct a character that means "to pretend" in Chinese? Let's look at an older style of clothing first!

 This picture can be used to signify **_clothes_**.

Let's use the progression

to reach the character, 衣 yī, that means "clothes" in Chinese.

Little girls love to dress up in front of the mirror.

The drawing 𝐐𝑓 or 𝐐𝑓 describes the scene. 〇 This drawing shows the mirror, 𝑓 shows two hands, and 𝐓 shows the dressing table. We could use the drawing, 工, as an abstraction or symbol of 𝐓 and 〇.

Let's use the progression

工 → 工 → ㅐ → ㅓ

to reach the symbol, ㅐ or ㅓ, which signifies "a mirror and the dressing table" here.

士 shì can be used to signify ㅅ.

By putting ㅐ or ㅓ, 士, and 衣 together, the character, 装(裝), signifies "a person sitting before a mirror and putting clothes on," therefore, 装(裝) zhuāng conveys the concept, "clothes."

It's possible that we could choose a costume and disguise ourselves to alter our appearance to pretend to be someone else. So, one of the extended meanings of 装(裝) zhuāng can be "to pretend."

to pretend	dead	to play dead	A person plays dead.
装(裝)	死	装死(裝死)	一人装死(一人裝死)
zhuāng	sǐ	zhuāng sǐ	yī rén zhuāng sǐ

You have learned (Simplified Chinese):

二人看到一只熊，一人立刻爬上树，另一人马上倒下装死。

... lìng yī rén mǎ shàng dǎo xià zhuāng sǐ。

...The other person immediately and purposely fell over down upon the ground to play dead.

用 yòng
to use; usefulness

How do we construct a Chinese character to express "to use?"

 This picture illustrates "washing a cup after using it or before using it."

Let's use the progression

to reach the character, 用 yòng, that is used to mean "to use" or "usefulness."

Note: *As shown below, the Chinese "full stop" (or "." in English) is a small circle "。".*

You have learned (Simplified Chinese):

二人看到一只熊，一人立刻爬上树，另一人马上倒下装死。熊用

... xióng yòng

... The Bear used

This shows an arrow that hits its target. Let's use the progression

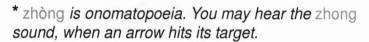

to reach the character, 中 zhòng*, that means "to hit the target."

* zhòng *is onomatopoeia. You may hear the* zhong *sound, when an arrow hits its target.*

中 zhōng (first tone) means "center" or "in the middle of." 中 is also short for "China."

In ancient China, to make decisions fortunetellers could apply an external heat source to a hole drilled earlier in a turtle shell. (We may hear the bǔ sounds in this process.)

The heat of which would cause the turtle shell to crack. Fortunetellers would interpret by observing the appearance of the crack. This whole process is symbolized as the character, 卜 bǔ, that means "divine" or "to foretell" in Chinese.

鼻 bí
nose

How do we construct a character that means "nose" in Chinese?

To understand why "nose" is written as 鼻 in Chinese, we should look at the nose from three different angles. We also take a look at the philtrum - the grooved area between the bottom of our nose and our upper lip.

Often Chinese people point to their own noses when saying "***myself***." The drawing, Ⳑ or 丂, is a sketch of the nose from 2 different angles. By putting Ⳑ on top of 丂, we get 自.

Let's use the progression

Ⳑ + 丂 → 自 → 自 → 自

to reach the symbol, 自 zì, that means "self."

We could use the symbol, 田, to signify a sketch of the nostrils part, ⬤, of the nose. 田 tián also means "farmland" in Chinese.
丌 is the abstraction of the philtrum.

By putting 自, 田, and 丌 together, the character, 鼻, is a brief drawing of a human nose. 鼻 bí means "nose" in Chinese.

However, because the pronunciation of 鼻 is bí, it's too short for people to hear and understand. So, 鼻 needs an auxiliary sound or character to help people to understand while listening. Let's introduce another character.

This shows a drawing of a child. Let's use the progression

→ 𝟛 → 孑 → 子

to reach the character 子 zi, which means "son" in Chinese, though it's also used as an auxiliary character sometimes.

By putting 鼻 and 子 together, 鼻子 bí zi (literally "the son of the nose") still means "nose" in Chinese.

You have learned:
二人看到一只熊，一人立刻爬上
树，另一人马上倒下装死。
熊用鼻子 xióng yòng bí zǐ

在 zài
at; in the process of

How do we construct a character to indicate "at (a location)" in Chinese?

If we break apart the character, 在, it contains three parts: ㇒, Ⅰ, and 土.
Let's find out the meaning of each part.

∭, ⺕, 大, or ㇒ This drawing signifies a sketch of a hand, according to ancient Chinese literature.

土 ──Plants growing from the earth
　──The surface of the earth
　──Earth

The character, 土 tǔ, is used to signify "earth" or "dirt."

止 This drawing can be used to signify "something hidden behind a dirt pile."

Now, by putting the ㇒, Ⅰ, and 土 together, 在 can be used to signify "a person's hand touching something hidden."

在？

In the process of finding and touching something hidden, thoughts that may go through a person's mind are "at (a location)," "in (a location)," or "to exist," so, 在 zài conveys the concept of "at (a location)," "in (a location)," or "to exist" in Chinese. One of the extended meanings of 在 is "in the process of."

一只熊在看人爬树。(一隻熊在看人爬樹。)
yī zhī xióng zài kàn rén pá shù
A bear was watching a person who was climbing into a tree.

You have learned (Simplified Chinese):
二人看到一只熊，一人立刻爬上树，另一人马上倒下装死。熊用鼻子在

liǎng rén kàn dào yī zhī xióng，yī rén lì kè pá shàng shù，lìng yī rén mǎ shàng dǎo xià zhuāng sǐ。xióng yòng bí zǐ zài

Two people saw a Bear. One person immediately climbed into a tree. The other person immediately threw himself flat down upon the ground to play dead. The Bear put its nose

她 tā
she; her

他 tā
he; him

How do we construct a character that means "she" in Chinese? Let's introduce the Chinese character for "female" first.

This drawing, or , shows a sketch of a female.
Let's use the progression

→ → 女

to reach the character, 女 nǚ,
which conveys the concept of "woman," "female," or "daughter."

If we see a person at a distance,

it may look like , , , 人, 人, or .

The character, 人 rén, is selected to mean "person" or "people." 女人 nǚ rén means "woman." Also, is used to signify "person" when is a component of another Chinese character.

෮ This illustrates the sketch of a snake. Let's use the progression

෮ → 也 → 也 → 也 → 也

to reach the character, 也 yě, that means "too" in Chinese. (When people first saw a cobra with its head raised off the ground, they soon realized that it was a snake, **too**.)

Let's now introduce the Chinese character 他. When someone or something suddenly appears nearby, the first question that usually goes through a person's mind is, "What is it?" When one realizes that it is another human, the idea that naturally presents itself is "human, too" or "he."

By putting 亻 and 也 together, we get 他 tā (he; him).

By putting woman 女 and 也 together, we get 她 tā (she; her).

You have learned (Simplified Chinese):

二人看到一只熊，一人立刻爬上树，另一人马上倒下装死。

熊用鼻子在他

... xióng yòng bí zǐ zài tā

的 de
possessive symbol;
adjective symbol

How do we construct a Chinese character to express "possession?"

In English, one way to form a possessive meaning is to add an apostrophe and an s at the end of a noun.

In Chinese, we **simply add the character** 的 to a noun, a phrase, or pronouns to form a possessive meaning.

This drawing illustrates the sketch of a light.

Let's use the progression

to reach the character, 白 bái, that is used to mean "bright" or "white."

ʃ or ʃ This drawing illustrates a sketch of a scoop. 勺 is the further modification of a scoop with a dot which signifies food or something inside the scoop. 勺 sháo, is used to mean "scoop."

We can use, 勺, to signify food. By putting 白

and 勺 together, the character 的 can be used to signify a person, carrying a light (白) in his right hand and some food (勺) in another hand, visited his friend and said to his friend "it's yours." So, the character, 的 de, conveys the concept, "possession."

In Chinese, we add the character 的 to a pronoun or noun to indicate possession.

* The character, 的 de, is the most commonly used characters. Statistic shows that we may see the character, 的 de, at least once, every time we read 25 Chinese characters on Chinese news paper.

You have learned:

二人看到一只熊，一人立刻爬上树，另一人马上倒下装死。熊用鼻子在他的

liǎng rén kàn dào yī zhī xióng，yī rén lì kè pá shàng shù，lìng yī rén mǎ shàng dǎo xià zhuāng sǐ。xióng yòng bí zǐ zài tā de

Two people saw a Bear. One person immediately climbed into a tree immediately. The other person immediately threw himself flat down upon the ground to play dead. The Bear put its nose to his

Because "I," "you," and "we" are used so often, we would like to introduce these Chinese characters to you in the following pages.

English	tree	above	person	the person in the tree
TC	樹	上	人	樹上的人
SC	树			树上的人

English	a person's nose/people's noses
Chinese	人的鼻子

English	a bear's nose/bears' noses
Chinese	熊的鼻子

English	a bear's nose	three bears' noses
TC	一隻熊的鼻子	三隻熊的鼻子
SC	一只熊的鼻子	三只熊的鼻子

You have learned:

二人看到一只熊，一人立刻爬上树，另一人马
上倒下装死。熊用鼻子在他的

Two people saw a Bear. One person climbed into a
tree immediately. The other person immediately threw
himself flat down upon the ground to play dead. The
Bear put its nose to his

**We have learned 她 and 他. Because " I," " you,"
and "we" are used so often, I would like to
introduce these Chinese characters to you in the
following pages.**

我 wǒ
I; me

How do we construct a character that means "I" in Chinese?

This is an ancient Chinese character that means "a hand."

These pictures show a hand from two different angles.

Let's use the progression

to reach the character, 手 shǒu, that means "a hand."

This drawing shows an ancient weapon with a tassel at one end.

This drawing, ⌐ or 弋, illustrates the abstraction of ⌐, so 弋 is used to signify a "weapon." The character, 戈 gē , means "halberd" in Chinese.

By putting 手 and 戈 together, 我 can be used

to signify "I hold a weapon." 我 wǒ is used to mean "I" or "me" in Chinese. 我的 wǒ de means "my."

我的手 wǒ de shǒu means "my hand."
我的二只手（我的二隻手）wǒ de liǎng zhī shǒu means "my two hands."

我看到的熊 wǒ kàn dào de xióng means "the bear I saw."

my nose	my bear	my horse
我的鼻子	我的熊	我的马（我的馬）
wǒ de bí zi	wǒ de xióng	wǒ de mǎ

my bear' nose	my horse's nose
我的熊的鼻子	我的马的鼻子（我的馬的鼻子）
wǒ de xióng de bí zǐ	wǒ de mǎ de bí zǐ

You have learned:
二人看到一只熊，一人立刻爬上树，另一人马上倒下装死。熊用鼻子在他的

liǎng rén kàn dào yī zhī xióng，yī rén lì kè pá shàng shù，lìng yī rén mǎ shàng dǎo xià zhuāng sǐ。xióng yòng bí zǐ zài tā de

Two people saw a Bear. One person immediately climbed into a tree. The other person immediately threw himself flat down upon the ground to play dead. The Bear put its nose

你 nǐ
you

How do we construct a Chinese character that means "you?" Let's see how Chinese people act while saying "you."

Often, some Chinese point their forefingers to others while saying "you."

👉, 👆, or 🤚 This drawing shows a sketch of this hand gesture.

Let's use the progression

👆 → 伊 → 尔 → 尔 → 尓 → 尔

to reach symbol, 尔, that can be used to signify "you" here.

As we learned earlier, 亻 signifies a person. By putting 亻 and 尔 together, we get 你 nǐ, that means "you" for both male and female.

In the story the goat is regarded as a male.

you	your	your nose	your bear	I saw your bear
你	你的	你的鼻子	你的熊	我看到你的熊
		nǐ de bí zi	nǐ de xióng	

⻖, ⺗, 忄, or 心 This drawing shows a sketch of a heart, and the character, 心 xīn, is used to mean "heart" or "mind" in Chinese. 忄 is the radical for "mind."

The word, 心上人, is a graceful way to mean a girl friend, a boy friend, darling, honey, or sweetheart. As a boy says "我的心上人 wǒ de xīn shàng rén," it means "my girl friend"; As a girl says "我的心上人," it means "my boy friend."

By putting 心 under 你, the character, 您 nín, is a polite way of addressing a person, you.

your another bear
你的另一只熊(你的另一隻熊)
nǐ de lìng yī zhī xióng

your another horse
你的另一只马(你的另一隻馬)
nǐ de lìng yī zhī mǎ

門 们 mén or men
a plural marker

In English, "they" is the plural form of "two or more people." Let's find out how the Chinese language system copes with this!

In Chinese, we simply **_add one character_** to a singular pronoun or noun to form a plural pronoun or noun. How? Let's find out.

This drawing shows a sketch of a saloon door.
Let's use the progression

田→門→門→门

to reach the character, 门(門) mén, that means "door."

As we learned earlier, 亻 is a radical for "person."

This sketch illustrates "two person standing in the doorway. **_They_** are talking about something."
Let's use the progression

⿰→⿰→倜→們→们

to reach symbol, 们(們) mén or men, that is used as a "plural marker." Interesting to see that 👣 looks like 門, to some extent.

The pronunciation of 们(們) mén is similar to the pronunciation of **man** in English. Both mén and men are appropriate and it depends on the speaker's mood or intention.
人们(人們) means "people." 我们(我們) means "we." 我们的(我們的) means "our."

You have learned:
二人看到一只熊，一人立刻爬上树，另一人马上倒下装死。熊用鼻子在他的

person/people	people	people's
人	人们	人们的

she	they/ them (female)	their (female)	he	they/ them (male)	their (male)
她	她们	她们的	他	他们	他们的

we/us	our/ours	our bear	our horse
我们	我们的	我们的熊	我们的马
		wǒ men de xióng	wǒ men de mǎ

I saw your bear was climbing a tree.
我看到你们的熊在爬树。
wǒ kān dào nǐ men de xióng zài pá shù

臉 脸 liǎn
face

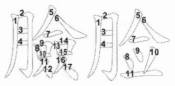

How do we construct a character that means "face" in Chinese?

月 or 月 This looks like a chunk of
pork hanging at a butcher's shop
and it also looks like a moon or a person's
body/back. The moon goes around the earth
monthly. 月 yuè is used to mean "moon" or
"month." 月 ròu is also used as a radical for
"meat," "flesh," or "body."

龠 or 僉 This can be used to illustrate a
person's face. Putting 月 and 僉 together, we
get the character 臉 liǎn, that means "face" in
Traditional Chinese.

This picture illustrates a person's face.

Let's use the progression

to reach the character, 脸 liǎn, that means
"face" in Simplified Chinese.

English	her face	his face	on her face
Pinyin	tā de liǎn	tā de liǎn	tā de liǎn shàng
TC	她的臉	他的臉	她的臉上
SC	她的脸	他的脸	她的脸上

English	my nose	my face
Pinyin	wǒ de bí zǐ	wǒ de liǎn
TC	我的鼻子	我的臉
SC		我的脸

English	two people's faces
Pinyin	liǎng rén de liǎn
TC	二人的臉
SC	二人的脸

You have learned:

二人看到一只熊，一人立刻爬上树，
另一人马上倒下装死。熊用鼻子在他的脸上

liǎng rén kàn dào yī zhī xióng　yī rén lì kè pá shàng
shù　lìng yī rén mǎ shàng dǎo xià zhuāng sǐ　xióng
yòng bí zǐ zài tā de liǎn shàng

Two people saw a Bear. One person climbed into a
tree immediately. The other person immediately threw
himself flat down upon the ground to play dead. The
Bear put its nose to his face

了 le   A function character to indicate
         a past tense
  liǎo   to understand; to finish

How do we construct a functional character to indicate "a past tense" in Chinese?

This drawing shows a sketch of a bow. Let's use the progression

$$D \rightarrow \} \rightarrow 弓 \rightarrow 了$$

to reach the character, 弓 gōng, which means "bow" in Chinese.

* *The* gōng sound is **onomatopoeia**. We may hear the gōng sound while an arrow is released from a powerful bow.

When a war has ended, the warriors were ready to return home, so they unstring their bows,).

The character, 了, can be used to signify "the end of a event" and 了 le can be used to act as a function character to indicate "a past tense."

了 liǎo is also used to convey the concept, "understand" or "finish."

聞 闻 wén
to hear;
to smell ;to sniff

How do we construct a character that means "to hear" in Chinese?

As we learned earlier, the character 门(門) mén means "door."

🦻 or This shows a sketch of an ear. Let's use the progression

to reach the character, 耳 ěr, that means "ear."

If someone is standing close to a door, this person is able to ***hear*** the noises coming from inside. If we signify this scene as "an ear in the doorway," such as 闻(聞).

The character, 闻(聞) wén, means "to hear."

Also, if we are standing at the door, we would be able to ***smell*** if someone was cooking a meal inside. Therefore, 闻(聞) wén also means "to smell" or "to sniff."

一只马闻了闻他的脸。(一隻馬聞了聞他的臉。)
yī zhī mǎ wén le wén tā de liǎn
A horse sniffed his face briefly.

我闻了闻他的脸。(我聞了聞他的臉。)
wǒ wén le wén tā de liǎn   I sniff ed his face.

我闻了闻马的脸。(我聞了聞馬的臉。)
wǒ wén le wén mǎ de liǎn   I sniff ed the horse's face.

马闻了闻我的脸。(馬聞了聞我的臉。)
mǎ wén le wén wǒ de liǎn   The horse sniffed my face.

一只熊闻了闻他的脸。
(一隻熊聞了聞他的臉。)
yī zhī xióng wén le wén tā de liǎn
A bear smelled his face briefly

* Here, in the sentence, the character, 闻(聞), is used twice,
闻了闻(聞了聞), to show the bear possibly didn't take it
seriously because the bear is not interested to eat dead person,
as people said.

You have learned:
二人看到一只熊，一人立刻爬上树，另一人马
上倒下装死。熊用鼻子在他的脸上闻了闻，

... xióng yòng bí zǐ zài tā de liǎn shàng wén le wén

... The Bear put its nose to his face, and sniffed briefly.

就 ^{jiù}
then

How do we construct a character for "then" in Chinese? Let's look at the sketch of a dog first!

, 犬, 犬, or 犬 This shows a sketch of a dog. We can see the dog's head, black nose, and 4 legs. So, 犬 quǎn is one of the characters which means "dog" in Chinese. If 犬 is a normal dog, the character, 尤, would seem like a special dog to us. So, 尤 yóu means "especially" in Chinese.

This shows a *tall* castle or a palace where the emperors lived, and it can be used to signify the *capital city*.

Let's use the progression

亭 → 京 → 京

to reach the symbol, 京, that signifies "high" and 京 jīng means "capital city" in Chinese.

In a capital city, while looking at a strange dog a thought that may go through a person's mind is "***success***."

If the capital city is old, it may not be what you expected. You may think to yourself, "Oh! I thought it was going to be different, but it's ***only*** like this," ***then*** you leave.

So, by putting 京 and 尤 together, 就 jiù conveys the concept, "success," "only," or "then."

他一看到熊，就立刻爬上树。
(他一看到熊，就立刻爬上樹。)
tā yī kàn dào xióng   jiù lì kè pá shàng shù
As soon as he saw the bear, he climbed into a tree right away.

You have learned:
二人看到一只熊，一人立刻爬上树，另一人马上倒下装死。熊用鼻子在他的脸上闻了闻就

liǎng rén kàn dào yī zhī xióng，yī rén lì kè pá shàng shù，lìng yī rén mǎ shàng dǎo xià zhuāng sǐ。xióng yòng bí zǐ zài tā de liǎn shàng wén le wén，jiù

...The Bear put its nose to his face, and sniffed briefly. Then

 zǒu
to walk

How do we construct a character that means "to walk"?

This picture illustrates a person is walking. We also can use the drawing, 大, to signify this scene. The second feature of the scene is the foot, 🦶.

Let's use the progression

to reach the character, 走 zǒu, that signifies "a person stretching out two legs to walk." 走 zǒu is used to mean "to walk." One of the extended meanings of 走 zǒu is "to leave" in Chinese.

You have learned:

二人看到一只熊，一人立刻爬上树，另一人马上倒下装死。熊用鼻子在他的脸上闻了闻就走了。

They left.	He left.	The bear left.
他们走了！	他走了！	熊走了。
tā men zǒu le	tā zǒu le	xióng zǒu le

躲 duǒ
to hide

How do we construct a character that means "to hide" in Chinese?

𠂉 This shows a side view of a human body. Let's use the progression

𠂉 → 𠂉 → 身 → 身 → 身 → 身

to reach the character, 身 shēn, which means "body."

As we learned earlier, 木 means "wood."
几 or 几 seems like "a person kneeling."
朵 This looks like a person 几 hiding in a tree. 朵 This can be used to signify "to hide." 耳朵 ěr duo also means "ear." 朵 duǒ is also a measure word for "flower."

By putting 身 and 朵 together, 躲 duǒ means "to hide" in Chinese.

You have learned:
二人看到一只熊，一人立刻爬上树，另一人马上倒下装死。熊用鼻子在他的脸上闻了闻，就走了。躲

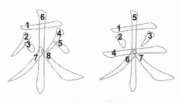

来 来 lái
to come

How do we construct a character that means "to come" in Chinese? Let's look at a wheat plant first!

This drawing illustrates a sketch of a wheat plant that is ready for harvest. It is at this time that many animals, birds, and people are ***drawn*** to it.
Let's use the progression

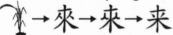

to reach the character, 来(來) lái, that means "to come."

below	Come!	Come down!
下	来(來)！	下来(下來)！

You have learned:

二人看到一只熊，一人立刻爬上树，另一人马上倒下装死。熊用鼻子在他的脸上闻了闻，就走了。躲在树上的人下来了，

... duǒ zài shù shàng de rén xià lái le，

... The person, hidden in the tree, came down.

问 问  wèn
to ask

How do we construct a character that means "to ask" in Chinese?

 As we learned earlier , 门(門) mén means "door" and 口 kǒu means "mouth" or "entrance."

Putting 门(門) and 口 together, 问(問)signifies "someone approaches a door, and opens his mouth." 问(問) wèn is used to mean "to ask."

In ancient China, 门(門) meant a "two piece door" and 户(戶) hù meant a "one piece door." Usually, the houses of the wealthy families or officials used the a two piece door, 门(門).

户(戶) hù is used to convey concept, "door," "a household or family (and also the legal term for same)," or "an account (in the bank)."

You have learned:
二人看到一只熊，一人立刻爬上树，另一人马上倒下装死。熊用鼻子在他的脸上闻了闻，就走了。躲在树上的人下来了，问

說说 shuō
to say;
to speak

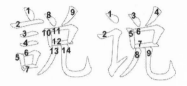

How do we construct a character that means "to say" in Chinese?

This shows a sketch of a speaking face. Let's use the progression

☺→言→讠

to reach the character, 言 yán, that is used to mean "to say" or "to speak." 言 is Simplified as 讠, when it is used as a radical in Simplified Chinese.

This is a picture of a person praying to gods with several sticks of incense. While praying, this person usually talks to the gods. This scene is often seen at temples in Asia.
Let's use the progression

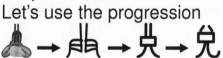

to reach the symbol, 兑, that can be used to signify "speak."
By putting 言/讠 and 兑 together, the character, 说(說)shuō, means "to say" or "to speak."

shén me
what

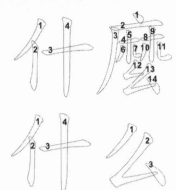

How do we express "what" in Chinese characters? Let's look at how people count first!

This drawing was used to signify "ten" in ancient China.

Later, people used ✚, ✛, or ╋ to signify "ten," because people knew better how to tie things together. Finally, the character, ╋ shí, is used to mean "ten" in Chinese.

If we see a person at a distance, it may look like 大, 人, 人, 亻, or 亻.

By putting 亻 and ╋ together, 亻╈, 亻╈, or 什 looks like a person, 亻, carrying ten things of something on his back. Therefore, 什 is used to means "varieties of things."

Let's use the component, 广, to represent a cave, or a place where ancient people could make a home.

As stated earlier, 木 means "wood" in Chinese. 木 also signifies "tree," 林 lín means "grove," and 森 sēn means "forest" in Chinese.

In ancient China, people brought fiber crops home for further processing to get fiber. By putting 广 and 林 together, the character, 麻 má, is used to mean "a family of plants which are used to make rope and strong rough cloth." 麻 is also used to convey the concept, "numerous."

 This drawing shows the drawing of a baby.

Let's use the progression

→ξ→ξ→幺→么

to reach the symbol, 幺 or 么 , that can be used to signify "the youngest" or "very small."

什么(什麼) shén me signifies "varieties of something" and "small," so it answers the question "**What**?" 什么(什麼) shén me means "What."

English	what	What did the bear say?
TC	什麼	熊說了什麼？
SC	什么	熊说了什么？
	shí me	xióng shuō le shí me

English	What did she say?	What did you say?
TC	她說了什麼？	你說了什麼？
SC	她说了什么？	你说了什么？
	tā shuō le shí me	nǐ shuō le shí me

You have learned:

二人看到一只熊，一人立刻爬上树，另一人马
上倒下装死。

熊用鼻子在他的脸上闻了闻，就走了。

躲在树上的人下来了，问："熊说了什么？"

liǎng rén kàn dào yī zhī xióng，yī rén lì kè pá shàng
shù，lìng yī rén mǎ shàng dǎo xià zhuāng sǐ。xióng
yòng bí zǐ zài tā de liǎn shàng wén le wén，jiù zǒu le。
duǒ zài shù shàng de rén xià lái le，wèn "xióng shuō le
shí me？"

...The Bear put its nose to his face, and sniffed briefly.
Then the bear went away.
Coming down from the tree, the person asked
"What did the Bear say to you?"

 dá
to answer

How do we construct a character that means "to answer" in Chinese?

This drawing illustrates a sketch of a facial expression while a person is **answer**ing people.

⌒ ⌒ This drawing shows a person's eyes and also shows the concentration of a person while talking.

⌒ This shows the crease that runs from the nose to the corner of the mouth. When people talk, often the crease appears on the face.

◯ This shows the opened mouth while speaking.

Let's use the progression

→ → 答

to reach the character, 答 dá, that means "to answer" in Chinese.

You have learned:

. . . 熊用鼻子在他的脸上闻了闻，就走了。躲在树上的人下来了，问："熊说了什么？" 答

 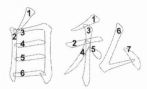

自 私 zì sī
selfish

How do we construct characters that mean "selfish" in Chinese? Let's look at how people use a symbol to express "private" first!

 This drawing shows a brief sketch of a wheat plant.

This drawing shows an abstraction of 𝑌.
This drawing signifies leaves growing upwards.
This drawing signifies "roots."
This drawing signifies hanging "grains."
Let's use the progression

𝑌 → 釆 → 禾

to reach the character, 禾, which signifies "crops" and the character, 禾 hé, is a general name for grain-bearing plant in Chinese.

Many people built fences, △, that surrounded their crops, 禾. Ancient Chinese used the symbol 厶 to signify a person's claim to crops.

Let's use the progression

to reach the character, 私 sī, that means "private" in Chinese.

As we learned the character, 鼻 bí, we also learned the character, 自 zì, that means "self."

The word 自私 zì sī is used to mean "selfish."

selfish person/ people	He is a selfish person.	You are selfish people.
自私的人	他是自私的人。	你是自私的人。
zì sī de rén	tā shì zì sī de rén	nǐ shì zì sī de rén

You have learned:

二人看到一只熊，一人立刻爬上树，另一人马上倒下装死。熊用鼻子在他的脸上闻了闻，就走了。

躲在树上的人下来了，问:"熊说了什么?"

答:"熊说 ： 自私的人

... duǒ zài shù shàng de rén xià lái le，wèn "xióng shuō le shí me ?" dá "xióng shuō : zì sī de rén

逃 táo
to flee

How do we construct a character that means "to flee" in Chinese? Let's look at how people run from danger!

朩, 氺, or 兆 This drawing looks like a brief sketch of "a person on the run."

辶 or 辶 This can be used to signify a person running so fast that it leaves a dust trail behind him.

Putting 辶 and 朩 together, the character, 逃 táo, is used to mean "to flee."

You have learned:

二人看到一只熊，一人立刻爬上树，另一人马上倒下装死。熊用鼻子在他的脸上闻了闻，就走了。躲在树上的人下来了，问:"熊说了什么?"

答:"熊说 : 自私的人逃的

... duǒ zài shù shàng de rén xià lái le，wèn "xióng shuō le shí me ?" dá "xióng shuō : zì sī de rén táo de

... Coming down from the tree, the person asked "What did the Bear say to you?" Answered, "The Bear said a selfish person fled away

快 kuài
quick

How do we construct a character that means "quick" in Chinese? Let's look at how people hold chopsticks when eating!

This drawing shows a sketch of a hand holding a pair of chopsticks while eating. Let's use the progression

𝄔 → ⼘ → ⼧ → ⾏ → 夫 → 夬

to reach the symbol, 夬, which signifies "a hand holding a pair of chopsticks while eating a meal."

While using chopsticks, we must concentrate our mind on the food at that moment. So we have to construct a symbol to express "mind" first.

Culturally, Chinese people associate the heart as "the source of thinking," so here we could construct the symbol for heart.

This drawing shows a simple sketch of a heart. Let's use the progression

💙 → ⼼ → ⼩ → 心 or 忄

to reach the symbol, 心 or 忄. The character, 心 xīn, means "heart" or "mind" in Chinese. 忄 is used as a radical for "mind."

Now, by putting 忄 and 夬 together, the character, 快 kuài, seems to show a person using chopsticks who enjoys eating and feeling happy. By using chopsticks people always try to get food *quick*ly. 快 is used to mean "quick" in Chinese.

He ran away fast.	He walks fast.
他逃的快 tā táo de kuài	他走的快 tā zǒu de kuài

快 走 ! kuài zǒu means "Walk quickly" or "Go away quicky!" (In China, a police may say to people 快 走 ! , when the police see a gathering and wants the people to go away.)

Most readers have seen chopsticks for a long time, so readers may be interested to know characters that mean "chopsticks" in Chinese.

⺮⺮ This drawing shows a photo of some bamboo leaves. Let's use the progression ⺮⺮ → 𠂉𠂉 → 竹 → 竹 → 竹 to reach the character, 竹 zhú, that means "bamboo" in Chinese. This drawing (竹) signifies "bamboo" when used as a component in a character, so 竹 is the radical for "bamboo." 竹 is often handwritten as 竹.

Now by putting 竹 and 快 together, 筷 kuài means "chopstick" or "chopsticks."

*kuài *is onomatopoeia, originating from the sound of of chopsticks colliding to each other. (Have you noticed that the pronunciation of 筷 is exactly the same as the pronunciation of 快? Have you noticed that 快 and* **quick** *share the same sound* k.)

However, because the pronunciation of 筷 is kuài, it's too short for people to hear and understand, so, 筷 often needs an auxiliary sound or character to help people to understand while listening.

As we learned the character 鼻子, we learned the character, 子 zi, can be used as an auxiliary character.

The word 筷子 kuài zi (literally "the son of the chopsticks") still means "chopstick" or "chopsticks."

你的筷子！
nǐ de kuài zǐ
Your chopsticks!

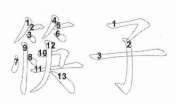

不 bú
   bù   no; not

How do we construct a character that means "no" in Chinese?

 This drawing shows a bird was taking off and flying away. The thought that may go through our mind is "It is gone. I could **not** catch it."

Let's use the progression

to reach the character, 不 bù or bú, that means "no" or "not" in Chinese.

When 不 *goes before a fourth-toned Chinese character in a phrase,* 不 *is pronounced* bú. *Otherwise,* 不 *is pronounced* bù.

You have learned:
答:"熊说:自私的人逃的快,不
... dá "xióng shuō : zì sī de rén táo de kuài , bú
... Answered, "The Bear said a selfish person fled away fast. ..not

是 shì
am; is; are; yes; was; were

How do we construct a character that means "is" in Chinese?

 This drawing shows a sketch of the sun. If we look at the sun through a pair of very dark sunglasses, the sun looks like this, ⊙.

Let's use the progression

☼ → ⊙ → ⊖ → 日 → 日

to reach the character, 日 rì, that means "sun" in Chinese.

or This drawing shows a sketch of a foot. We could use the symbol, , to signify a person. This can be used to signify a person walking *right* towards a target.

Let's use the progression

to reach the character, 正 zhèng, which indicates "progressive tense," and means "correct," "right", or "positive" in Chinese.

We can use this drawing to signify that a person is walking under the scorching sun. At that moment the thought running through his mind could be "**Yes**, I am heading for my destiny."

Let's use the progression

是→是→是→是

to reach the character, 是 shì, that is used to mean "yes," "is," "am," "is," "are," "was," or "were," in Chinese.

** Have you noticed that the pronunciation of 是 shì is very similar to the pronunciation of **s** in English **is**?*

not	am/is/are/was/were	am not/is not/are not/was not/were not
不	是 shì	不是 bú shì

It's me.	It's not me.	It's mine.	It's not mine.
是我	不是我	是我的。	不是我的。
shì wǒ	bú shì wǒ	shì wǒ de	bú shì wǒ de

You have learned:

. . . 答:"熊说:自私的人逃的快，不是

... dá "xióng shuō : zì sī de rén táo de kuài，bú shì

... Answered, "The Bear said a selfish person fled away fast. He is not

好 hǎo
good; fine

Most Chinese may say: "Lovely baby! _Good_!" when they see a mother holding a baby.

 This photo shows a woman holding a baby. As a Chinese watches the scene, the immediate thought that may go through her or his mind is "***good***."

Let's use the progression

to reach the character, 好 hǎo, which means and conveys the concept of "good" or "fine" in Chinese. ┡┪ This drawing signifies "two hands holding the baby."

As we learned earlier, the character, 女 nǔ, means and conveys the concept of "woman" "female," or "daughter" in Chinese.

Also we learned earlier, the character, 子 zǐ or zi, means and conveys the concept of "son" in Chinese.

朋友 péng yǒu
friend

How do we construct a word that means "friend" in Chinese? "Friends follow the same leader, and friends work together for the same goal." Let's observe the ancient phoenix bird!

When a phoenix flew in the sky, tens of thousands of other birds came and gathered, according to ancient Chinese literature. Many birds followed the same leader, flew together, and they were ***friends***.

This drawing was used to illustrate the above scene in ancient Chinese literature.

Let's use the progression

朝 → 翔 → 羽 → 彡 → 朋 → 朋

to reach the character, 朋 péng, which means and conveys the concept of "friend." Have you noticed that 月 looks like the shape of human's back and 朋 looks like "two friends standing together" or "many birds"?

* Have you noticed that the pronunciation of 朋 is the

same as the sound of huge birds flapping their wings?

Also friends go together, because of the same goal. ⅀ This drawing illustrates two hands or signifies two people work together for the same goal.

Let's use the progression

⅀ → 乎 → 龙 → 龙 → 友 → 友

to reach the character, 友 yǒu, that also means and conveys the concept of "friend (work together with others for the same goal)."

朋友 péng yǒu is often used to mean "friend" or "friends" in modern Chinese.

You have learned:

二人看到一只熊，一人立刻爬上树，另一人马上倒下装死。熊用鼻子在他的脸上闻了闻，就走了。躲在树上的人下来了，问:"熊说了什么?"
答:"熊说:自私的人逃的快，不是好朋友。"

... dá "xióng shuō : zì sī de rén táo de kuài，bú shì hǎo péng yǒu。

... Answered, "The Bear said that a selfish person fled away fast. He is not a good friend."

You are my good friend.	You are my good friends
你是我的好朋友。	你们是我的好朋友。
nǐ shì wǒ de hǎo péng yǒu	nǐ men shì wǒ de hǎo péng yǒu

與 与 _{yǔ}
and

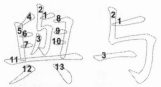

How do we construct a character that means "and" in Chinese? Let's observe "how people work together!"

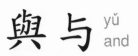 This drawing illustrates a sketch of a plant in a field "＿".

This sketch illustrates two people, **A** and **B**, are looking after the plant together, which obviously conveys the concept of "and" or "participation."

Let's use the progression

$$ \text{🖑} \rightarrow \text{𦥔} \rightarrow \text{𦥑} \rightarrow \text{與} \rightarrow \text{與} \rightarrow \text{𠂉} \rightarrow \text{与} $$

to reach the character, 与(與) yǔ, that conveys the concept, "and."

You have learned:

two men and the bear	you and me	The bear and the horse
二人与熊	你与我	熊与马
liǎng rén yǔ xióng	nǐ yǔ wǒ	xióng yǔ mǎ

You and I are good friends.	You and I are good friends.
你与我是好朋友。	你是我的好朋友。
nǐ yǔ wǒ shì hǎo péng yǒu	nǐ shì wǒ de hǎo péng yǒu

Congratulations! You have learned many Chinese characters one by one, now you should be able to read and understand the following story completely in Chinese.

Title: 二人與熊 (Traditional Chinese)

二人看到一隻熊，一人立刻爬上樹，另一人馬
上倒下裝死。

熊用鼻子在他臉上聞了聞，就走了。

躲在樹上的人下來了，問:"熊說了什麼?"

答:"熊說：自私的人逃的快，不是好朋友。"

Characters also learned in the book: 三目土至能刀巴
爪木力口歹衣卜中自田子女也他她白勺戈你心
您門們月弓耳犬尤京身言十林森麻禾竹筷日正

Title: 二人与熊 (Simplified Chinese)

二人看到一只熊，一人立刻爬上树，另一人马
上倒下装死。

熊用鼻子在他脸上闻了闻，就走了。

躲在树上的人下来了，问:"熊说了什么?"

答:"熊说:自私的人逃的快，不是好朋友。"

Characters also learned in the book: 三目土至能刀巴
爪木力口歹衣卜中自田子女也他她白勺戈你心
您门们月弓耳犬尤京身言十林森麻禾竹筷日正

Pronunciation

liǎng rén kàn dào yī zhī xióng，yī rén lì kè pá shàng shù，lìng yī rén mǎ shàng dǎo xià zhuāng sǐ。xióng yòng bí zǐ zài tā de liǎn shàng wén le wén，jiù zǒu le。

duǒ zài shù shàng de rén xià lái le，wèn："xióng shuō le shí me ?" dá："xióng shuō：zì sī de rén táo de kuài，bú shì hǎo péng yǒu。

Title: Two Men and The Bear

Two people saw a Bear. One person immediately climbed into a tree. The other person immediately and purposely fell over down upon the ground to play dead.

The Bear put its nose to his face, and sniffed briefly. Then the bear went away.

Coming down from the tree, the person asked "What did the Bear say to you?"

Answered, "The Bear said a selfish person fled away fast. He is not a good friend."

Two Men and The Bear

Pronunciation
Reference
Chinese-Pinyin-MPS

☞ **Check out this interesting book available for kids and parents.**

ISBN: 1439265062

两只老虎
(兩隻老虎)

Simplified Chinese 两只 老虎　　两只 老虎
Traditional Chinese (兩隻 老虎　　兩隻 老虎)
Two　tigers,　two　　tigers,
跑 得 快　　跑 得 快
(跑 得 快　　跑 得 快)
run　fast,　run　　fast!

一只 没有 耳朵　一只 没有 尾巴
(一隻 沒有 耳朵　一隻 沒有 尾巴)
One doesn't have ears. One doesn't have a tail.

真 奇 怪　　真 奇 怪
(真 奇 怪　　真 奇 怪)
Really strange!　Really strange!

liǎng zhī lǎo hǔ liǎng zhī lǎo hǔ
pǎo de kuài　pǎo de kuài
yì zhī méi yǒu ěr duo
yì zhī méi yǒu wěi ba (yǐ ba)
zhēn qí quài zhēn qí quài

Pronunciation Reference

Page	Chinese	Pinyin	Tone	MPS
				(MPS: Mandarin Phonetic System)
3	一	yī, yí, yì	1,2,4	ㄧ, ㄧˊ, ㄧˋ
3	二	èr, liǎng	4,3	ㄦˋ, ㄌㄧㄤˇ
3	三	sān	1	ㄙㄢ
5	人	rén	2	ㄖㄣˊ
6	看	kàn	4	ㄎㄢˋ
6	目	mù	4	ㄇㄨˋ
7	到	dào	4	ㄉㄠˋ
7	土	tǔ	3	ㄊㄨˇ
7	至	zhì	4	ㄓˋ
8	熊	xióng	2	ㄒㄩㄥˊ
8	能	néng	2	ㄋㄥˊ
9	隻 只	zhī	1	ㄓ
11	立	lì	4	ㄌㄧˋ
11	刻	kē, kè	1,4	ㄎㄜ, ㄎㄜˋ
11	刀	dāo	1	ㄉㄠ
13	爪	zhuǎ	3	ㄓㄨㄚˇ
13	爬	pá	2	ㄆㄚˊ

Learning Chinese The Easy Way

Pronunciation Reference

Page	Chinese	Pinyin	Tone	MPS
				(MPS: Mandarin Phonetic System)
13	巴	bā	1	ㄅㄚ
14	上	shàng	4	ㄕㄤˋ
14	下	xià	4	ㄒㄧㄚˋ
15	樹 树	shù	4	ㄕㄨˋ
15	木	mù	4	ㄇㄨˋ
17	另	lìng	4	ㄌㄧㄥˋ
17	口	kǒu	3	ㄎㄡˇ
17	力	lì	4	ㄌㄧˋ
18	馬 马	mǎ	3	ㄇㄚˇ
20	倒	dǎo	3	ㄉㄠˇ
22	死	sǐ	3	ㄙˇ
22	歹	dǎi	3	ㄉㄞˇ
23	裝 装	zhuāng	1	ㄓㄨㄤ
23	衣	yī	1	ㄧ
25	用	yòng	4	ㄩㄥˋ
25	卜	bǔ	3	ㄅㄨˇ
25	中	zhōng	1	ㄓㄨㄥ

Pronunciation Reference

Page	Chinese	Pinyin	Tone	MPS
				(MPS: Mandarin Phonetic System)
27	鼻	bí	2	ㄅㄧˊ
27	子	zǐ, zi	3,5	ㄗˇ, ㄗ·
27	自	zì	4	ㄗˋ
27	田	tián	2	ㄊㄧㄢˊ
29	在	zài	4	ㄗㄞˋ
31	她	tā	1	ㄊㄚ
31	女	nǔ	3	ㄋㄩˇ
31	他	tā	1	ㄊㄚ
31	也	yě	3	ㄧㄝˇ
32	的	de	5	ㄉㄜ·
32	白	bái	2	ㄅㄞˊ
32	勺	sháo	2	ㄕㄠˊ
36	我	wǒ	3	ㄨㄛˇ
36	戈	gē	1	ㄍㄜ
38	你	nǐ	3	ㄋㄧˇ
38	妳	nǐ	3	ㄋㄧˇ
39	您	nín	2	ㄋㄧㄣˊ

Pronunciation Reference

Page	Chinese		Pinyin	Tone	MPS
					(MPS: Mandarin Phonetic System)
40	們	们	**mén, men**	2,5	ㄇㄣˊ, ㄇㄣ·
40	門	门	**mén**	2	ㄇㄣˊ
42	臉	脸	**liǎn**	3	ㄌㄧㄢˇ
42	月		**yuè**	4	ㄩㄝˋ
44	弓		**gōng**	1	ㄍㄨㄥ
44	了		**le**	5	ㄌㄜ·
45	聞	闻	**wén**	2	ㄨㄣˊ
45	耳		**ěr**	3	ㄦˇ
47	就		**jiù**	4	ㄐㄧㄡˋ
47	犬		**quǎn**	3	ㄑㄩㄢˇ
47	尤		**yóu**	2	ㄧㄡˊ
47	京		**jīng**	1	ㄐㄧㄥ
49	走		**zǒu**	3	ㄗㄡˇ
50	躲		**duǒ**	3	ㄉㄨㄛˇ
50	身		**shēn**	1	ㄕㄣ
51	來	来	**lái**	2	ㄌㄞˊ
52	問	问	**wèn**	4	ㄨㄣˋ

Pronunciation Reference

Page	Chinese		Pinyin	Tone	MPS
					(MPS: Mandarin Phonetic System)
53	說	说	shuō	1	ㄕㄨㄛ
53	言		yán	2	ㄧㄢˊ
54	什		shén	2	ㄕㄣˊ
54	麼	么	me	5	ㄇㄛ˙
54	十		shí	2	ㄕˊ
55	林		lín	2	ㄌㄧㄣˊ
55	森		sēn	1	ㄙㄣ
55	麻		má	2	ㄇㄚˊ
57	答		dá	2	ㄉㄚˊ
58	自		zì	4	ㄗˋ
58	私		sī	1	ㄙ
58	禾		hé	2	ㄏㄜˊ
60	逃		táo	2	ㄊㄠˊ
61	快		kuài	4	ㄎㄨㄞˋ
61	心		xīn	1	ㄒㄧㄣ
61	筷		kuài	4	ㄎㄨㄞˋ
64	不		bú	2	ㄅㄨˊ

Pronunciation Reference

Page	Chinese	Pinyin	Tone	MPS
				(MPS: Mandarin Phonetic System)
64	不	bù	4	ㄅㄨˋ
64	卜	bǔ	3	ㄅㄨˇ
65	是	shì	4	ㄕˋ
65	日	rì	4	ㄖˋ
65	正	zhèng, zhēng	4,1	ㄓㄥˋ, ㄓㄥ
67	好	hǎo	3	ㄏㄠˇ
67	子	zǐ, zi	3,5	ㄗˇ, ㄗ·
68	朋	péng	2	ㄆㄥˊ
68	友	yǒu	3	ㄧㄡˇ
70	與 与	yǔ	3	ㄩˇ

Learning Chinese The Easy Way
(Traditional & Simplified Characters)
Story 2

The Wind and The Sun

风　与　太阳

風　與　太陽

★Unveil the **foundation** of Chinese characters!

The first story, **Two Men and The Bear**,
contains the following characters.

<u>Traditional Chinese:</u>
二人看到一隻熊，一人立刻爬上樹，另一人馬
上倒下裝死。
熊用鼻子在他臉上聞了聞，就走了。
躲在樹上的人下來了，問:"熊說了什麼?"
答:"熊說：自私的人逃的快，不是好朋友。"
Characters also learned in the book: 三目土至能刀巴
爪木力口歹衣卜中自田子女也他她白勺戈你心
您門們月弓耳犬尤京身言十林森麻禾竹筷日正

<u>Simplified Chinese:</u>
二人看到一只熊，一人立刻爬上树，另一人马
上倒下裝死。
熊用鼻子在他脸上闻了闻，就走了。
躲在树上的人下来了，问:"熊说了什么?"
答:"熊说:自私的人逃的快，不是好朋友。"
Characters also learned in the book: 三目土至能刀巴
爪木力口歹衣卜中自田子女也他她白勺戈你心
您门们月弓耳犬尤京身言十林森麻禾竹筷日正

In the story, The Wind and The Sun, only new
characters will be introduced in detail.

風风 fēng
wind

How do we construct a character that means "wind" in Chinese?

To cope with cold windy days, ancient Chinese may use mesh nets to (partially) block the **wind**. We can use the diagram, Π or Π, to signify a net.

Naturally, over time, some insects (𝑀) may get caught in the net. Let's use the progression
𝑀 → 血 → 血 → 虫 → 虫 → 玉
to reach the character, 虫 chóng, that means "insect" or "worm" in Simplified Chinese and used almost by every Chinese, though academically, 蟲 chóng is the Traditional Chinese. The line, —, (at the top of the 玉) represents a string that the insect has held on to. Putting Π, — and 虫 together, 風 fēng means "wind" in Traditional Chinese. 风 fēng means "wind" in Simplified Chinese.

* *The* fēng sound is **onomatopoeia**. We may hear the fēng sound while listening to a strong wind. *The* fèng sound is pronounced like the English word, **phone**.

You have learned: 风　fēng　The Wind

與 与 yǔ
and

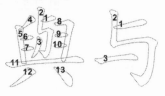

We have learned the character, 与(與), earlier.

人与熊(人與熊) rén yǔ xióng means "human and bear."

我与我的好朋友(我與我的好朋友) wǒ yǔ wǒ de hǎo péng yǒu means "my good friends and me."

我与她是好朋友。(我與她是好朋友。)
wǒ yǔ tā shì hǎo péng yǒu
She and me are good friends.

我与她不是好朋友。(我與她不是好朋友。)
wǒ yǔ tā bú shì hǎo péng yǒu
She and I are not good friends.

我与人人是好朋友。(我與人人是好朋友。)
wǒ yǔ rén rén shì hǎo péng yǒu
I am everyone's good friends.

As a general rule, the pronunciation of the traditional character and the simplified character for any specific Chinese character is the same. So, 風 and 风 have the same pronunciation, fēng; 與 and 与 have the same pronunciation, yǔ.

太陽　tài yáng
太阳　sun

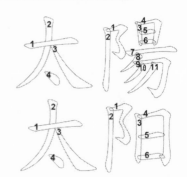

How do we construct the characters that mean "sun" in Chinese?

大 大 大 These are brief sketches of a person, with outstretched arms signifying something big. Ancient Chinese thought the sky, earth, and humans were all "big." The character, 大 dà, is ued to mean "big" in Chinese.

If we add one "dot" to 大, we get 太 tài that means "extreme" in Chinese. Also, 太 means "extremely" or "excessively" in Chinese.

大门(大門) dà mén means "main gate" or "gate."

大人 dà rén can be used to mean "adult" or used to address a judge or any high official respectfully.

一只熊爬上大树(一隻熊爬上大樹。)
yī zhī xióng pá shàng dà shù
A bear climbed into a big tree.

二人看到一只大熊，一人立刻爬上大树。
(二人看到一隻大熊，一人立刻爬上大樹。)
liǎng rén kàn dào yī zhī dà xióng yī rén lì kè pá shàng dà shù
Two people saw a big bear. One person immediately climbed into a big tree.

Both **大快人心** dà kuài rén xīn and **人心大快** rén xīn dà kuài mean "to the satisfaction of everyone" or " to the great satisfaction of the public." (When to use **大快人心**. For example, if a very bad person died, many people may say **他的死，大快人心！**)

大森林 dà sēn lín means "the big forest."

大风(大風) dà fēng means "the strong wind."
风水(風水) fēng shuǐ means "feng shui."
In ancient China, wind and rain affected people's life very much.

风太大(風太大) fēng tài dà means "the wind is too strong."

他的大鼻子 tā de dà bí zi means "His big nose."
他的鼻子大 tā de bí zi dà means "His nose is big."

熊的大手 xióng de dà shǒu means "The bear's big hand."
大熊的手 dà xióng de shǒu means "The big bear's hands."

他用大刀 tā yòng dà dāo means "He used a big knife."

她是我的太太。
tā shì wǒ de tài tài   She is my wife.

太太 means "wife." (This is one way to say "wife.")

我的太太是她。

wǒ de tài tài shì tā   My wife is her.

☼ This drawing shows "a **sun** rises over mountains." We can use the drawing, 〥, to signify "sunray through woods." We can see a tree and "sunray."

Let's use the progression

to reach the character, 阳(陽) yáng, means "sun." 阳(陽) yáng also conveys the extended concept, "male," "positive," or "yang." The character, 日, is a radical for "sun."

The pronunciation of 阳(陽) yáng is too short for people to hear and understand, so 太阳(太陽) tài yáng is used to mean "sun."

太好了！tài hǎo le means "Excellent!" or "Very good!"

You have learned:

风与太阳

fēng yǔ tài yáng

The Wind and The Sun

正
zhèng
a character indicating progressive tense; positive; right

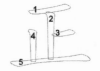

正月 zhēng yuè means "January."

正门(正門) zhèng mén means "the front main gate."

正好 zhèng hǎo means "at the right moment" or "just right."

正心 zhèng xīn means "to set right one's mindset."

风能(風能) fēng néng means "wind energy."
能力 néng lì means "ability" or "potentiality."

太阳能(太陽能) tài yáng néng or 日光能 rì guāng néng mean "solar energy."

熊正用鼻子在你脸上闻。
(熊正用鼻子在你臉上聞。)
xióng zhèng yòng bí zǐ zài nǐ liǎn shàng wén
The bear is sniffing your face.
In the sentence, the character, 正, is short for 正在.

You have learned:
风与太阳正
fēng yǔ tài yáng zhèng

在 zài
at; in the process of

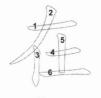

他在看什么?（他在看什麼?）
tā zài kàn shí me
What is he looking at? or What is he reading?

你在看什么?（你在看什麼?）
nǐ zài kàn shí me
What are you looking at? (What are you reading?)

他在不在? tā zài bú zài can mean "Is he alive or dead?", " Is he at home, or not?", or " Is he in office, or not?"

正在 zhèng zài means "in the process of."

大白熊正在看你的脸。
（大白熊正在看你的臉。）
dà bái xióng zhèng zài kàn nǐde liǎn
The big white bear was watching your face.

他正在说什么?（他正在說什麼?）
tā zhèng zài shuō shí me
What is he saying?

You have learned:
风与太阳正在
fēng yǔ tài yáng zhèng zài

☞ Traditional or Simplified Chinese first?

For the most commonly used Chinese characters, Simplified Chinese keeps more than 70% of the Traditional Chinese characters; for the remaining 30% of the Simplified Chinese characters, most of them look like the simplified version of their Traditional Chinese characters.

In this book, readers easily learn both Simplified Chinese characters and Traditional Chinese characters in two popular Chinese stories, and, readers get the overall picture of of Chinese written language.

On the other hand, frankly speaking, even Chinese get confused if they try to learn both Simplified and Traditional characters simultaneously.

Because Simplified characters are used in China by more than 1.3 billions Chinese, many readers like to learn Simplified characters first. For readers who want to study Chinese medicine or ancinet Chinese literature should learn Traditional characters first.

(If you visit famous temples in China or any Chinese societies, often you can see some Traditional Chinese characters there, because China is a nation with a deeply rooted culture: Traditional Chinese characters have been used in China several thousand years, while the Simplified Chinese characters are used in China only after 1956.)

争争 zhēng
to contend

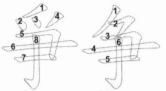

How do we construct a character that means "to contend" in Chinese? Let's observe how people fight for something.

This drawing shows a sketch of a hand. Let's use the progression

to reach the symbol, ㄋ, ㄇ, or ㄣ, that can be used to signify "a hand."

This drawing can be used to signify "two people who are contending for something." Let's use the progression

to reach the character, 争(爭) zhēng, that conveys the concept, "to contend," "to argue," or "struggle."

他们在争什么?(他們在爭什麼?)
tā men zài zhēng shí me
What are they arguing about? or What are they fighting for?

You have learned:
风与太阳正在争
fēng yǔ tài yáng zhèng zài zhēng

 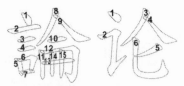

論 论 lùn
to discuss;
a theory

How do we construct a character that means "to discuss" in Chinese?

While discussing a topic, people speak and sift through ideas.

As we learned earlier, the character, 言 yán, means "to say" or "to speak" in Chinese. 言 is simplified as 讠, when it is used as a radical in Simplified Chinese.

Gills are what fish use to get oxygen from the water, so they can breathe.
🐟 or 🐚 This illustrates a sketch of gills.
Let's use the progression

to reach the symbol, 仑(侖) lún, which can be used to signify "to sift through ideas" or "logical order."

Putting 言 and 侖 together,
the character, 論 lùn, that means "to discuss"

or "discussion" in Traditional Chinese.

Putting 讠 and 仑 together, the character, 论 lùn, that means "to discuss" or "discussion" in Simplified Chinese.

在争论中，他走了！
(在爭論中，他走了！)
zài zhēng lùn zhōng tā zǒu le
He left after a dispute.

他们在争论什么？
(他們在爭論什麼？)
tā men zài zhēng lùn shí me
What are they arguing about?

他们二人在争论什么？
(他們二人在爭論什麼？)
tā men liǎng rén zài zhēng lùn shí me
What are these two people arguing about?

风与太阳正在争论什么？
(風與太陽正在爭論什麼？)
fēng yǔ tài yáng zhèng zài zhēng lùn shí me
What are Wind and Sun arguing about?

You have learned:
风与太阳正在争论
fēng yǔ tài yáng zhèng zài zhēng lùn

力量 lì liàng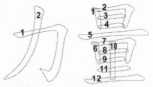
power

How do we construct the characters that mean "power" in Chinese? Let's first take a look at the common plow!

As we learned earlier, 力 lì, means "strength." Two of the extended meanings of 力 lì is "force" or "power."

水力 shuǐ lì means "hydraulic power."

How do we construct a character to describe the capacity of power in Chinese? Let's look at an old scale first!

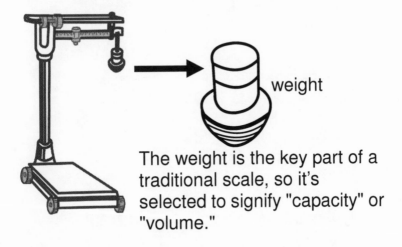

weight

The weight is the key part of a traditional scale, so it's selected to signify "capacity" or "volume."

Let's use the progression

to reach the character, 量 liàng, which conveys the concept, "amount," "quantity," or "estimate."

By putting 力 and 量 together, 力量 signifies "the amount of strength," so 力量 lì liàng means "power" or "strength" in Chinese.

大量 dà liàng conveys the concept, "a lot," in Chinese.

这只熊的力量好大。
(這隻熊的力量好大。)
zhè zhī xióng de lì liàng hǎo dà   This bear is very powerful.
力量大 lì liàng dà means "powerful" in Chinese.

他的力量好大。
tā de lì liàng hǎo dà   His strength is very powerful.

You have learned:
风与太阳正在争论   力量大
fēng yǔ tài yáng zhèng zài zhēng lùn   lì liàng dà

誰 谁 shuí or shéi
who; whom

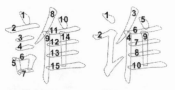

How do we construct a character that means "who" in Chinese?

▦ This drawing shows a sketch of a gate.

冊 or 隹 We could use this drawing to signify "a visitor is waiting outside the gate and waving his hand."

By putting speak 言 / 讠 and 隹 together, the character, 谁(誰) shuí, can be used to signify "W**ho** is it?" when a host sees a visitor outside. 谁(誰) shuí means "who" or "whom." (Some Chinese pronounce 谁(誰) as shéi.)

谁?(誰?) shuí means "Who is it?"

你是谁?(你是誰?) nǐ shì shuí means "Who are you?"

她是谁?(她是誰?) tā shì shuí means "Who is she?"

是谁来看你?(是誰來看你?) shì shuí lái kàn nǐ or
来看你的是谁?(來看你的是誰?) lái kàn nǐde shì shuí means "Who was the person who came to see you?"

You have learned:
风与太阳正在争论谁
fēng yǔ tài yáng zhèng zài zhēng lùn shuí

的 dì target
de possessive symbol;
adjective symbol

谁是看门的人？(誰是看門的人？)
shuí shì kàn mén de rén
Who is the gatekeeper?

看门的人是谁？(看門的人是誰？)
kàn mén de rén shì shuí

谁的力量大？(誰的力量大？)
shuí de lì liàng dà   Who is more powerful?

是谁爬上了树？是谁逃走了？
(是誰爬上了樹？是誰逃走了？)
shì shuí pá shàng le shù shì shuí táo zǒu le
Who was the person to climb into the tree?
Who was the person to flee away?

是谁与谁在争论？(是誰與誰在爭論？)
shì shuí yǔ shuí zài zhēng lùn
Who are the people arguing?

是谁与谁在争论什么？
(是誰與誰在爭論什麼？)
shì shuí yǔ shuí zài zhēng lùn shí me
What are they arguing about?

他来看马的目的是什么？
(他來看馬的目的是什麼？)
tā lái kàn mǎ de mù dì shì shí me

What's his purpose, to come and see the horse?

目 的 mù dì means "goal," "intention," or "purpose."

他来看你的目的是什么？
(他来看你的目的是什麽？)
tā lái kàn nǐde mù dì shì shí me
What's his purpose, to come and see you?

熊闻他的脸目的是什么？
(熊聞他的臉目的是什麽？)
xióng wén tā de liǎn mù dì shì shí me
What's the brear's purpose, to sniff his face?

你的目的是不是来看看大熊？
(你的目的是不是來看看大熊？)
nǐde mù dì shì bú shì lái kàn kàn dà xióng
Whether your purpose is to come and see the big bear?

(Though **大熊** usually means "big bear," **大熊** can also be
used as a male's nick name. This person may loke like a bear or
his surname is **熊**. Whether it is a bear or a person's nick name,
we have to read the context.)

* The character, **的**, is the most commonly used characters.

Statistic shows that we may see the character, **的**, more then 3
times, when we read 100 Chinese characters on Chinese news
paper.

You have learned:
风与太阳正在争论谁的力量大。
fēng yǔ tài yáng zhèng zài zhēng lùn shuí de lì liàng dà。
The Wind and the Sun were arguing which one was more
powerful.

这 这 zhè
this

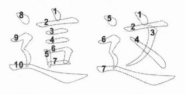

How do we construct a character that means "this" in Chinese?

This drawing illustrates a person walking and pointing at the ground saying, "***This*** is the place." At some point in our lives, it is likely someone we know has done this.

The key concepts of the above illustration are: ***foot***, ***walk***, ***speak*** (言 or 讠), and ***this***.

辶 or 辶 This shows a person running so fast that it leaves a dust trail behind him. We can use 辶 to signify ***walk***.

Let's use the progression

to reach the character, 这(這) zhè, that means "this." 这人(這人) zhè rén means "this person."

这只熊是谁的?
(這隻熊是誰的?)
zhè zhī xióng shì shuí de   Whose bear is this?

这只熊的力量好大。
(這隻熊的力量好大。)
zhè zhī xióng de lì liàng hǎo dà   This bear is very powerful.
力量大 lì liàng dà means "powerful" in Chinese.

这只熊好快就爬上了大树！
(這隻熊好快就爬上了大樹！)
zhè zhī xióng hǎo kuài jiù pá shàng le dà shù
Very quickly this bear climbed into the big tree!

这只熊用鼻子在他脸上闻了闻，就走了。
(這隻熊用鼻子在他臉上聞了聞，就走了。)
zhè zhī xióng yòng bí zǐ zài tā liǎn shàng wén le wén jiù zǒu le
This bear put its nose to his face, and sniffed briefly. Then the bear went away.

这只熊是我的！(這隻熊是我的！)
zhè zhī xióng shì wǒ de
This bear is mine.

这是我的熊！(這是我的熊！)
zhè shì wǒ de xióng
This is my bear.

You have learned:
风与太阳正在争论谁的力量大。这
fēng yǔ tài yáng zhèng zài zhēng lùn shuí de lì liàng
dà。zhè

時时 shí
time

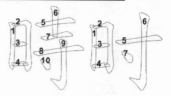

How do we construct a character that means "time" in Chinese?

Earlier we learned the character, 日 rì, that means "sun" or "day."

This picture illustrates a traditional Chinese temple, which is very much related to *time*, because before Chinese people go to temples, they often try to find the best *time* to visit temples. The character, 寺 sì means "temple" in Chinese.

Let's use the progression

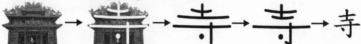

to reach the character, 寺 sì means "temple" in Chinese.

We can use the character, 日, to signify "people try to find the best *time* to visit temples." Putting 日 and 寺 together, 時 shí, is used to mean "time" in Traditional Chinese.

The character, 時 shí, is simplified as 时 shí in Simplified Chinese.

We may see the character, 寸, contained in other characters.

⟨hand image⟩ or ⟨hand image⟩ shows the hand and the black dot "●" where the Chinese doctors feel the pulse. Let's use the progression

⟨progression of characters⟩

to reach the character, 寸 cùn, that signifies "heart," because what the doctor gets from the pulse-taking is the beating or throbbing of the heart. Culturally Chinese people associate the heart with "the source of thinking" or "mind," so, 寸 is used as a radical for "mind."

A pulse is small, so 寸 is also used as a radical to signify "small" or "humble."

寸 cùn is also used to represent "the distance between where the Chinese doctors feel the pulse and the hand" or "a unit of length equal to one-third of a decimeter."

三时正(三時正) ān shí zhèng means "3 o'clock sharp."

他们二人正在争论谁的力量大，这时，熊来了。
(他們二人正在爭論誰的力量大，這時，熊來了。)

tā men liǎng rén zhèng zài zhēng lùn shuí
de lì liàng dà zhè shí xióng lái le

When these 2 people were arguing about who was more
powerful, the bear came.

二人看到一只熊，这时，一人立刻爬上树，另
一人马上倒下装死。
(二人看到一隻熊，這時，一人立刻爬上樹，另
一人馬上倒下裝死。)

liǎng rén kàn dào yī zhī xióng zhè shí   yī rén lì kè pá
shàng shù   lìng yī rén mǎ shàng dǎo xià zhuāng sǐ

Two people saw a Bear. At the time, one person immediately
climbed into a tree, and, the other person immediately and
purposely fell over down upon the ground to play dead.

风与太阳正在争论谁的力量大。就在这时，一
人走来。(風與太陽正在爭論誰的力量大。就在
這時，一人走來。)

fēng yǔ tài yáng zhèng zài zhēng lùn shuí de lì liàng
dà   jiù zài zhè shí   yī rén zǒu lái

The Wind and the Sun were arguing which one was
more powerful. Exactly at this moment, they saw a
person walking down the road.

You have learned:
风与太阳正在争论谁的力量大。
这时，   ... zhè shí   ... At this moment,

行 xíng　to walk; ok
　　háng　a shop; a firm

How do we construct characters that convey the concept, "a pedestrian"?

卝 This shows the sketch of an intersection. Let's use the progression

卝 → 彳亠 → 行

to reach the character, 行 xíng, which conveys the concept, "to walk." 行 xíng is also used to convey the concept, "ok," "to circulate," "to distribute," "to be popular," "able," "competent," "to do," "to carry out," "to conduct," and "behavior." 行人 xíng rén means "a pedestrian" or "pedestrians."

This picture illustrates two shoppers in front of a *shop*.
Let's use the progression

圃 → 冊 → 亻行 → 彳行 → 行

to reach the character, 行 háng, that conveys the concept, "a shop" or "a firm."

外行人 wài háng rén means "a layman."
力行 lì xíng means "to proceed with determination."

行人

这只熊是谁的？(這隻熊是誰的？)

zhè zhī xióng shì shuí de　Whose bear is it?

☞

As we learned earlier, 十 shí, means "ten" and the character, 一, means one. Putting 十 on the top of 一, 士, can be used to signify "a wise person who was able to count from 1 to 10," so, 士 shì, conveys the concept, "a learned person."

You have learned:

风与太阳正在争论谁的力量大。

这时，他们看到一　行人

...zhè shí, tā men kàn dào yī　xíng rén

At this moment, they saw a　pedestrian

 gè

How do we construct measure word for people in Chinese?

 This shows the sketch of a human body with internal organs.

Let's use the progression

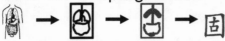

to reach the character, 固 gù, which has been used to mean and convey the concept of "solid" in Chinese, 固, because a body is sealed all around and stuffed inside.

We learned earlier the character, 亻 is a radical for person. By putting 亻 and 固 together, the Traditional Chinese character, 個 gè, has been used as "a measure word for objects, such as: people, families, buildings, ideas, schools, etc..." 個 gè is also informally used as a measure word for many other objects, such as: heads, melons, eggs, etc..., though those objects have formal measure words.

* A measure word is used to denote the form or shape of an item. For example, in English we can say a slice of bread or a loaf of bread, but we can't say, "a bread." Generally, in Chinese all nouns, both countable and uncountable, require measure word just as "bread" does in English.

 This picture shows a Terra Cotta soldier in battle armor.

The left character is an ancient Chinese oracle bone script, which can be used to signify "a soldier in armor."

Let's use the progression

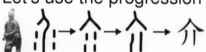

to reach the character, 介 jiè, which conveys the concept of "to serve as intermediary."
人 This drawing looks like "the armor on two shoulders" or "a person."

In ancient China, 介 jiè was used as a measure word for soldiers and people. Now the simplified Chinese character, 个 gè, is used as the Simplified Chinese version of the Traditional Chinese character, 個 gè.

	one pedestrian yī gè xíng rén	two pedestrians liǎng gè xíng rén	three pedestrians sān gè xíng rén
TC	一個行人	二個行人	三個行人
	1 個行人	**2** 個行人	**3** 個行人
SC	一个行人	二个行人	三个行人
	1 个行人	**2** 个行人	**3** 个行人

一只熊看到二个人，二个人也看到了熊。
(一隻熊看到二個人，二個人也看到了熊。)
yī zhī xióng kàn dào liǎng gè rén liǎng gè rén yě kàn dào le xióng
A bear saw 2 people. These two people also saw the bear.

十来个人看到了熊！(十來個人看到了熊！)
shí lái gè rén kàn dào le xióng
More than 10 people saw the bear.

快来看！一只熊！(快來看！一隻熊！)
kuài lái kàn　yī zhī xióng
Come quickly!　A bear!

You have learned:
风与太阳正在争论谁的力量大。
这时，他们看到一个行人

fēng yǔ tài yáng zhèng zài zhēng lùn shuí de lì liàng
dà。zhè shí，tā men kàn dào yī gè xíng rén

The Wind and the Sun were arguing which one was
more powerful. At this moment, they saw a pedestrian

走　zǒu
to walk

这时，他们看到一个路人。
(這時，他們看到一個路人。)
zhè shí tā men kàn dào yī gè lù rén
At this moment, they saw a person walking on road.
路人 lù rén means "a person walking on road" or "people walking on road."

走开！(走開！) zǒu kāi means "Go away!"
(A police may say this to a bystander or bystanders of a riot.)

他走了！
tā zǒu le　He has left!
(他走了！ can be used to mean "He died." It's more graceful to say 他走了！ than 他死了！.)

他走了？　　　　他走了！
Has he left?　　　He has left!

他走了？
tā zǒu le　Has he left?
(Sometimes, with the little help of the facial impression, we may change the intonation of a sentence from an assertive sentence in the simple present tense into an interrogative sentence. The above is an example.)

路 lù
road; path

How do we construct a character that means "road" in Chinese? Let's look at a foot first!

 This drawing shows a sketch of a foot. Let's use the progression

to reach the symbol, 足, that signifies "foot."

This drawing shows a construction worker working at a highway construction site.

This shows a sketch of the above scene, while 𠂤 signifies the hand with a tool.

Let's use the progression 𠂤 → 各 → 各

to reach the symbol, 各, which signifies "road" here. (Actually, 各 gè is a character, which could be used to mean "each," "every," "respectively," or "individually.")

By putting 足 and 各 together, 路 lù means "road" or "path" in Chinese.

上 shàng
above; upper

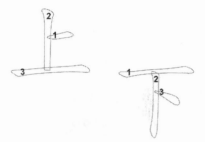

下 xià
below; lower

车来了，快上车！(車來了，快上車！)
chē lái le kuài shàng chē
The vehicle has arrived. Get on the vehicle quickly.
(We will learn the character, 车(車), in the the story, The Fox
and The Goat. 车(車) means "vehicle.")

到了，到了，下车！(到了，到了，下車！)
dào le dào le xià chē
We have arrived. We have arrived. Let's get off the vehicle!

他看来三十上下。(他看來三十上下。)
tā kàn lái sān shí shàng xià
He looks like around thirty years old.

他上个月来看她。(他上個月來看她。)
tā shàng gè yuè lái kàn tā   He came to visit her last month.
上月 shàng yuè also can be used to mean "last month."

他上上个月来看她。(他上上個月來看她。)
tā shàng shàng gè yuè lái kàn tā
He came to visit her the month before last month.

下个月(下個月) xià gè yuè means "next month."
下月 xià yuè also can be used to mean "next month."

說说

shuō
to say;
to speak

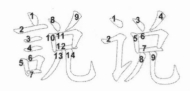

他说了什么？你说了什么？
(他說了什麼？你說了什麼？)
tā shuō le shí me   nǐ shuō le shí me
What did he say?   What did you say?

他说他看到了你的好朋友。
(他說他看到了你的好朋友。)
tā shuō tā kàn dào le nǐ de hǎo péng yǒu
He said he saw your good friend.

你在说什么？(你在說什麼？)
nǐ zài shuō shí me   What are you talking about?

谁说是你说的？(誰說是你說的？)
shuí shuō shì nǐ shuō de   Who said you said it?

他说他只是一个路人。
(他說他只是一個路人。)
tā shuō tā zhǐ shì yī gè lù rén
He said he is only a passerby.

You have learned:

风与太阳正在争论谁的力量大。 这时，他们看
到一个行人走在路上，太阳说："谁
... tā men kàn dào yī gè xíng rén zǒu zài lù shàng , tài
yáng shuō : "shuí

能
néng
can; ability; energy

你能不能来？（你能不能來？）
nǐ néng bù néng lái   Can you come or not?

他说了他能来！（他說了他能來！）
tā shuō le tā néng lái   He said he could come.

他说他不能来！（他說他不能來！）
tā shuō tā bù néng lái   He said he couldn't come.

他说他只能来一下！（他說他只能來一下！）
tā shuō tā zhǐ néng lái yī xià
He said he can only come and stay for a little while.

(Here, 只 means "only.")

他的能力 tā de néng lì means "his ability."

You have learned:

风与太阳正在争论谁的力量大。

这时，他们看到一个行人走在路上，太阳说："

谁能 fēng yǔ tài yáng zhèng zài zhēng lùn shuí de lì
liàng dà。 zhè shí，tā men kàn dào yī gè xíng rén zǒu
zài lù shàng，tài yáng shuō："shuí néng
... the Sun said: "Whichever of us can

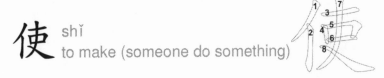

使 shǐ
to make (someone do something)

How do we construct a character that means "to make (someone do something)" in Chinese? Let's look at the character 吏 first!

If we break apart the character 吏, it contains three parts: 一, 口 and 乂.

We could use 一 to signify a hat or "government authority, and 口 this signifies a sketch of ancient government documents.

ψ This drawing shows a sketch of a hand. Let's use the progression ψ → ⺈ → 乂 to reach the symbol, 乂, that signifies a "hand" here.

By putting 一, 口 , and 乂 together, 吏 signifies "*an government official* holding documents," so, the character, 吏 lì , means "a government official" in Chinese.

By putting 口 and 乂 together, 史 signifies *documents* being held by a hand, and, the character, 史 shǐ, can be used to mean "history" in Chinese. As a matter of fact, 史 was a title name in ancient China given to the person responsible for writing down all the emperor's activities. He would write without bias, even when under pressure from authorities.

Now we will look at the character, 使.

丿 or 亻 This shows a sketch of a person, so 亻 signifies "human." By putting 亻 and 吏 together, 使 shǐ could be used to mean "to make (someone) do something" or "an envoy" in Chinese.

大使 dà shǐ means "ambassador."

big	envoy	tā shì gè dà shǐ He is an ambassador.
大	使	他是个大使。(他是個大使。)

大使来看你了。(大使來看你了。)
dà shǐ lái kàn nǐ le The ambassador comes to see you.

谁能使熊走开？(誰能使熊走開？)
shuí néng shǐ xióng zǒu kāi
Who can make the bear go away?

You have learned:

... 这时，他们看到一个行人走在路上，太阳说："谁能使

脱 tuō
to take off (clothes)

How do we construct a character that means "to take off (clothes)" in Chinese? Let's look at how people take off their clothes first!

This drawing shows a person taking off his shirt. We could use this drawing, 儿, as the abstraction of the above drawing.

Let's use the progression 儿 ➙ 儿 ➙ 兑

to reach the symbol, 兑, that can be used to signify "to take off (clothes)" here.

月 or 月 This looks like a chunk of pork hanging at a butcher's shop and it also looks like a moon. The moon goes around the earth monthly. So, we could use 月 ròu to signify "meat," "flesh," or "body." Also, the character, 月 yuè, means "moon" or "month" in Chinese.

By putting 月 and 兑 together, the character, 脱 tuō, has been invented to mean and convey the concept of "to take off (clothes)" in Chinese.

衣服 yīfú
clothes

How do we construct the characters that mean "clothes" in Chinese?

This picture can be used to signify *clothes*.

Let's use the progression

to reach the character, 衣 yī, that means "clothes" in Chinese.

However, partly because the pronunciation of 衣 yī is too short for people to hear and understand, so, there is a need to construct another character, 服, to go with 衣 to mean "clothes" to remove ambiguity.

If we break apart the character 服, it contains three parts: 月, 卩, and 又.

Because 月 is a component of 服, it signifies the character, 服, is related to human body.

This drawing shows a sketch of a shirt.

Let's use the progression

to reach the symbol, 卩, which can be used to signify "clothes."

 This drawing shows a sketch of a hand.

Let's use the progression

to reach the symbol, 又, , which can be used to signify "a hand."

By putting 月, 卩, and 又 together, the character, 服 fú, is used to convey the concept, "clothes" in Chinese.

衣服 yīfú means "clothes."

脱下衣服 yīfú means "to take off clothes."

这是谁的衣服？(這是誰的衣服？)

zhè shì shuí de yīfú Whose clothes are these?

his clothes	my clothes	your clothes
他的衣服	我的衣服	你的衣服
tā de yīfú	wǒ de yīfú	nǐde yīfú

You have learned:

... 这时，他们看到一个行人走在路上，太阳说："谁能使行人脱下衣服，谁

就 jiù
exactly

这时，谁来看他，谁就是他的好朋友。

(這時，誰來看他，誰就是他的好朋友。)

zhè shí shuí lái kàn tā shuí jiù shì tā de hǎo péng yǒu

Now, anyone who comes to see him is his good fiend.
(Probably he is in difficulties.)

一... 就

他一看到你，就逃走了。

tā yī kàn dào nǐ jiù táo zǒu le

He ran away as soon as saw you.

他一看到熊，就逃走了。

tā yī kàn dào xióng jiù táo zǒu le

He ran away as soon as he saw the bear.

熊一看到你，就逃走了。

xióng yī kàn dào nǐ jiù táo zǒu le

The bear ran away as soon as he saw you.

熊一看到人，就逃走了。

xióng yī kàn dào rén jiù táo zǒu le

The bear ran away as soon as he saw a human being.

我一爬上树，熊就到了树下。

(我一爬上樹，熊就到了樹下。)

wǒ yī pá shàng shù xióng jiù dào le shù xià

The bear arrived under the tree as soon as I climbed into the tree.

他一看到熊走了，就爬下树。
(他一看到熊走了，就爬下樹。)
tā yī kàn dào xióng zǒu le jiù pá xià shù
He came down from the tree as soon as he saw the bear left.

我一来，就看到你。(我一來，就看到你。)
wǒ yī lái jiù kàn dào nǐ
I saw you as soon as I came.

他马上就到了。(他馬上就到了。)
tā mǎ shàng jiù dào le
He will arrive very soon.

我马上就好。(我馬上就好。)
wǒ mǎ shàng jiù hǎo   I'll be ready very soon.

你一到，他就来看你。(你一到，他就來看你。)
nǐ yī dào tā jiù lái kàn nǐ
He will come to see you as soon as you arrive.

他不是好人，人们一看到他，就说他。
(他不是好人，人們一看到他，就说他。)
tā bú shì hǎo rén   rén men yī kàn dào tā   jiù shuō tā
He is not a good person. People criticize him as soon as see him.

You have learned:
...太阳说："谁能使行人脱下衣服，谁就力量大。
...   tài yáng shuō："shuí néng shǐ xíng rén tuō xià yī fú shuí jiù lì liàng dà
... the Sun said: "Whichever of us can cause him to take off his clothing shall be regarded as more powerful."

藏　cáng
　　to hide

How do we construct a character that means "to hide" in Chinese? Let's think about what we do when hiding something.

When we were kids, while thinking about hiding something, we might think of maybe hiding it "in the grass" or "in a wall or above the ceiling" where it would be protected. After hiding it we may look at it every day to see whether it's still there. Here we mentioned, "grass," "wall," "ceiling," "eye," and "protect."

ᐯᐯ This drawing shows a sketch of grass. Let's use the progression

ᐯᐯ ➝ ᐯᐯ ➝ ++ ➝ ⧺

to reach the character, ⧺, which signifies "grass." For any character with such a component "⧺," it means this character is related to grass, or (more generally), plants.

彐 This drawing shows a brief sketch of a wall.

彐⌐ This drawing shows a brief sketch of "wall and ceiling."

⿰ This drawing shows a sketch of a watching eye, while 臣 looks like the abstraction of ⿰.

⿰ or ⿰ This shows the abstraction of an ancient weapon ⿰ with a tassel at one end.

Now, by putting 艹, 疒, 臣, and ⿰ together, 藏 signifies "to hide something in a wall or above the ceiling, in the grass, to keep watch over it and to protect it ." The character, 藏 cáng, is used to mean "to hide" or "to store." The abbreviation of Tibet in Chinese is 藏 zàng.

树上藏了三个藏人。(樹上藏了三個藏人。)
shù shàng cáng le sān gè zàng rén
There are 3 Tibetans hiding in the tree.
藏人 zàng rén means "Tibetan."

一路上，我看到三个藏人。
(一路上，我看到三個藏人。)
yī lù shàng wǒ kàn dào sān gè zàng rén
On the way I saw 3 Tibetans.

他一看到熊，就立刻爬上树，藏在树上。
(他一看到熊，就立刻爬上樹，藏在樹上。)
tā yī kàn dào xióng jiù lì kè pá shàng shù cáng zài shù shàng
He climbed into a tree and hid there as soon as he saw the bear.

You have learned:
太阳藏 tài yáng cáng   Sun hid

烏乌 _{wū}

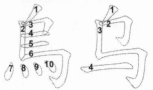

a color name (as black as
a crow's color); a crow

How do we construct a character to express a crow's color?

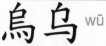 This drawing shows a sketch
of a bird.

Let's use the progression

to reach the character, 乌(鳥) niǎo,
that means "bird."

A crow also is a bird. The difference is that the crow is unique for its black color, its ***eyes are hardly visible***, and people can't see its eyes. Therefore, the character, 乌(烏) wū, is a short name for "crow." The character, 乌(烏) wū, is used to describe the color which is similar to black but not really the same—such as the color of a crow, a storm cloud, a dirty river, the beautiful hair of a girl, etc.

How do we construct a character for "black."

This drawing shows a sketch of a fire.

Let's use this progression 灬→ 火 → 火
to reach the character, 火 huǒ, which means
"fire."

火力 huǒ lì means "thermodynamic power."

The character, 黑, means "black" in Chinese.
Let's see why.

Here is a picture of a smoking
chimney. Apparently there are flames
of fire underneath and black chimney
dust inside the chimney.

This picture is the abstraction of the
above. It shows fire and soot exiting
into the air via a chimney. •••• This
signifies "burning ashes."

Let's use the progression

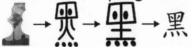

to reach the character, 黑 hēi, means "black."

You have learned:

... 这时，他们看到一个行人走在路上，太阳说：
"谁能使行人脱下衣服，谁就力量大。太阳藏在
乌

雲云 yún
cloud

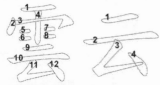

How do we construct a character that means "cloud"?

⌇ This shows a brief sketch of a cloud.

Let's use the progression

⌇ → ⌇ → ⌇ → 云

to reach the symbol, 云, which signifies "cloud."

▥ This drawing signifies "rain."
Let's use the progression

▥ → 雨 → 雨 → 雨

to reach the character, 雨 yǔ, that means "rain."

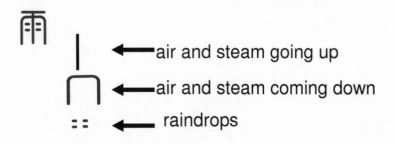

雨

| ←——air and steam going up

∏ ←——air and steam coming down

∷ ←—— raindrops

下雨了 xià yǔ le means "It has been raining."

走在雨中的人看到了我。
zǒu zài yǔ zhōng de rén kàn dào le wǒ
The person walking in the rain saw me.

在风雨中，他来看我。
(在風雨中，他來看我。)
zài fēng yǔ zhōng tā lái kàn wǒ
In the rain and wind, he came to see me.

在风雨中，我的朋友来看我。
(在風雨中，我的朋友來看我。)
zài fēng yǔ zhōng wǒ de péng yǒu lái kàn wǒ
In the rain and wind, my friend came to see me.

黑云来了，快下雨了！(黑雲來了，快下雨了！)
hēi yún lái le kuài xià yǔ le
Because the black cloud is coming, it will rain soon.

Putting 雨 on top of 云, the character, 雲 yún, means "cloud" in Traditional Chinese.
The character, 云 yún, means "cloud" in Simplified Chinese.

You have learned:
太阳藏在乌云

tài yáng cáng zài wū yún

the Sun hid ... the dark cloud

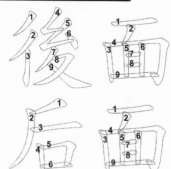

後面 hòu miàn
后面 behind

How do we construct the characters to express "behind" in Chinese?

This drawing can be used to signify "a person, with a baby on his shoulders, is **behind** another person."

If we see a person at a distance, it may look like this: 人 or ⸀.
Let's use the progression

人 ➜ ⸀ ➜ 亻 ➜ two people 仃 ➜ 彳

to reach the character, 彳, that can be used to signify "a person is behind another person" or "behind" here.

 This shows a drawing of a baby.
Let's use the progression

🧒 ➜ 8 ➜ ໊ ➜ ໌ ➜ 幺

to reach the symbol, 幺, which can be used to signify a "baby" or a "burden" on someone.

☞   夊

This picture shows a patient is receiving acupuncture treatment, which takes longer time to complete, comparatively.

This picture can be used to signify the above drawing. Also we can use this drawing, 夊 or 夊, to signify this acupuncture treatment. This drawing, 夊, can be used to signify "left behind."

Putting 彳, 幺, and 夊 together, 後 can be used to signify "walk slowly" or "left behind." The character, 後 hòu, is used to mean "behind" in Traditional Chinese. One of the extended meanings of 後 is "offspring."

▬▬▬▬▬▬▬▬▬

 This ancient Chinese character means "queen." The modern writing is 后. So,

后 means "queen" in Chinese.

ʃ This drawing looks like a graceful lady.

一 This can be used to signify "to give
ɾ order," while ɾ signifies "a mouth."

An ancient Chinese queen only hid **behind** in the palace. The character, 后 hòu, is used to mean "behind" in Simplified Chinese.

However, because the pronunciation of 后(後) hòu is too short for people to hear and understand, often 后面(後面) has been used to mean "behind." Let's learn the character, 面.

⊞ This shows the sketch of a face and hair.

The rectangular area of ⊞ shows the important part of a face: the eyes and the nose. Let's use the progression

to reach the character, 面 miàn, which means "the face of a person" or "surface."

后面(後面) hòu miàn (literally the back part of

something) is used to mean "behind" or "at the back" in Chinese.

太阳藏在乌云后面(太陽藏在烏雲後面)
tài yáng cáng zài wū yún hòu miàn means "The Sun hid behind the dark cloud."

后人(後人) hòu rén means "offspring."

后来(後來) hòu lái means "later on."

她一个月后来看你。(她一個月後來看你。)
tā yī gè yuè hòu lái kàn nǐ
She will come to see you one month later.

我的朋友看到熊，立刻爬上树，我马上倒下装死，后来，熊在我的脸上闻了闻，就走了。
(我的朋友看到熊，立刻爬上樹，我馬上倒下裝死，後來，熊在我的臉上聞了聞，就走了。)
wǒ de péng yǒu kàn dào xióng   lì kè pá shàng shù
wǒ mǎ shàng dǎo xià zhuāng sǐ   hòu lái   xióng zài
wǒ de liǎn shàng wén le wén   jiù zǒu le

You have learned:
... 太阳藏在乌云后面，
tài yáng cáng zài wū yún hòu miàn
... the Sun hid behind the cloud,

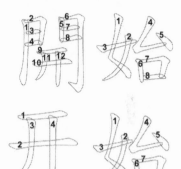

開始
开始

kāi shǐ
to start

How do we construct the characters that mean "to start"?

Earlier we learned that 門 means "door."

▯ or 干 This can be used to symboloze closed curtains.

开 This can be used to symboloze "opening up," "to start," or "to open."

Let's use this progression

門开 → 門开 → 開 → 开

to reach the symbol, 开(開) kāi, that is used to mean "to start" or "to open."

走开！(走開！) zǒu kāi means "Go away!"

你走开！(你走開！) nǐ zǒu kāi means "You! Go away!"

你们走开！(你們走開！) nǐ men zǒu kāi means "You all! Go away!"

开水(開水) kāi shuǐ means "boiled water."

白开水(白開水) bái kāi shuǐ means "plain boiled water."

水开了！(水開了！) shuǐ kāi le means "Water is boiling!"

开口(開口) kāi kǒu can be used to mean "open mouth, break silence."

后来，他开口了！(後來，他開口了!)
hòu lái tā kāi kǒu le
Later on, he started to talk."

开火！(開火！) kāi kǒu means "Open fire (in battle)!"

开刀(開刀) kāi dāo means "to operate in surgery."

开门(開門) kāi mén means "Open the door!"

开开门(開開門) kāi kāi mén
(If this sentence was spoken softly, it usually means "Please open the door!" If this sentence was spoken strongly and very loud, it usually means "Open the door (immediately)!")

看到你，我好开心！(看到你，我好開心！)
kàn dào nǐ   wǒ hǎo kāi xīn
I am so happy to see you!
Here, 开心(開心) means "happy, enjoying happy moment."

In modern Chinese conversation, 开(開) and 始 often go together to mean "to start," so here we will learn the character, 始.

Let's break apart the character 始 directly by its three parts: 女, 厶, and 口. Let's find out the meaning of each part.

As we learned, the character, 女 nǚ, means "female," "woman," or "daughter" in Chinese. Obviously, because every person came from his/her mother, so, 女, can be used to signify "to begin."

∪ This could be used to symboloze a sketch of a food container.
Let's use the progression
∪ → 凵 → 厶
to reach the symbol, 厶, which can be used to symboloze a finished meal or indicate "it's time to begin a new job."

▽ or 口 This shows a sketch of a mouth, so, 口 kǒu, means "mouth" or "entrance" in Chinese. 口 This also can be used to symboloze "beginning."

Putting 女, 厶, and 口 together, the character, 始 shǐ, means "beginning" or "start" in Chinese.

开始(開始) kāi shǐ means "to start" or "to begin."

一开始，熊看看我，后来，熊闻了闻我，就走了。
(一開始，熊看看我，後來，熊聞了聞我，就走了。)
yī kāi shǐ　xióng kàn kàn wǒ　hòu lái　xióng wén le
wén wǒ　jiù zǒu le
In the begining, the bear looked at me, then, the bear sniffed me
briefly and left.

人们一开始争论，他就走了。
（人們一開始爭論，他就走了）
rén men yī kāi shǐ zhēng lùn　tā jiù zǒu le
As soon as people start arguing, he left.

一看到你，我就开心！
(一看到你，我就開心！)
yī kàn dào nǐ　wǒ jiù kāi xīn
As soon as seeing you, I became happy!

大风一来，就开始下大雨了！
(大風一來，就開始下大雨了！)
dà fēng yī lái　jiù kāi shǐ xià dà yǔ le
As soon as strong winds start to blow, the heavy rain starts!

You have learned:
...这时，他们看到一个行人走在路上，太阳说：
"谁能使行人脱下衣服，谁就力量大。"
太阳藏在乌云后面，风开始
... "tài yáng cáng zài wū yún hòu miàn　fēng kāi shǐ
... the Sun hid behind the dark cloud, and the Wind
began

用 yòng
to use; usefulness

他说："这刀太大，不好用！"
(他說："這刀太大，不好用！")
tā shuō　zhè dāo tài dà　bù hǎo yòng
He said the knife is too big to use.

他说："这刀中看不中用！"
(他說："這刀中看不中用！")
tā shuō　zhè dāo zhōng kàn bù zhōng yòng
He said : "the knife looks appealing, but it is useless."

他问："这刀好用不好用？"
(他問："這刀好用不好用？")
tā wèn　zhè dāo hǎo yòng bù hǎo yòng
He asked: "Is this a good knife to use?"

熊用鼻子闻他的手。(熊用鼻子聞他的手。)
xióng yòng bí zǐ wén tā de shǒu
The bear put its nose to his hand and sniffed his hand.

他们只用太阳能与风能。
(他們只用太陽能與風能。)
tā men zhǐ yòng tài yáng néng yǔ fēng néng
They only use solar enegy and wind enegy.

用户（用戶）yòng hù means "subscriber to electric power,
telephone, etc."

You have learned:
... 太阳藏在乌云后面，风开始用力

 chuī
to blow

How do we construct a character that means "to blow" in Chinese?

This sketch shows air coming out of a mouth.

Let's use the progression

to reach the symbol, 欠, that signifies "to blow air."

口 This is a sketch of a mouth, so 口 means "mouth" or "entrance." Putting 口 and 欠 together, the character, 吹 chuī, means "to blow."

风用力吹。（風用力吹。）
fēng yòng lì chuī   The Wind blows hard.

You have learned:
... 太阳藏在乌云后面，风开始用力吹，

... "tài yáng cáng zài wū yún hòu miàn fēng kāi shǐ yòng lì chuī
... the Sun hid behind the dark cloud, and the Wind began to blow hard

刮 guā
to scrape

How do we construct a character that means "scrape"?

 This shows a brief sketch of a tongue. Let's use the progression

舌 → 舌 → 舌 → 舌 → 舌

to reach the character, 舌 shé, that means "tongue."

三寸舌 sān cùn shé is used to describe a great talker.

火舌 huǒ shé is used to describe the flame of a fire.

As we learned earlier, 刀 dāo means "knife." 刂 is used as a radical for "knife."

Now, by putting 舌 and 刂 together, 刮 signifies, "to remove by scraping from the surface of an object by a sharp knife(or a tool)," therefore, the character, 刮 guā , means "to scrape."

The character, 吹 and 刮, are different. We use 刮 here as a measurement, or how hard the wind is blowing. At times, the wind can blow so hard it may feel like you are a plant caught in a grain thresher.

他用刀刮下手上的土。tā yòng dāo guā xià shǒu shàng de tǔ means "He used a knife to scrape away dirt from his hand."

黑云来了，马上就开始刮风下雨了！
(黑雲來了，馬上就開始刮風下雨了!)
hēi yún lái le　mǎ shàng jiù kāi shǐ jǐ fēng xià yǔ le
Because the black cloud is coming, strong winds may begin to blow and rain may begin to fall soon.

You have learned:
风与太阳正在争论谁的力量大。这时，他们看
到一个行人走在路上，太阳说："谁能使行人脱
下衣服，谁就力量大。" 太阳藏在乌云后面，
风开始用力吹，风刮的

fēng yǔ tài yáng zhèng zài zhēng lùn shuí de lì liàng
dà。zhè shí，tā men kàn dào yī gè xíng rén zǒu zài lù
shàng，tài yáng shuō："shuí néng shǐ xíng rén tuō xià
yī fú shuí jiù lì liàng dà。" tài yáng cáng zài wū yún
hòu miàn，fēng kāi shǐ yòng lì chuī，fēng guā de
The Wind and the Sun were arguing which one was more powerful. At this moment, they saw a pedestrian walking down the road, and the Sun said: "Whichever of us can cause him to take off his clothing shall be regarded as more powerful." So the the Sun hid behind the dark cloud, and the Wind began to blow hard upon the man. The Wind blew...

越 yuè
to jump over; more

How do we construct a character that means "more" in Chinese?

If we break apart the character 越, it contains two parts: 走 and 戉.

ʔ 𝆑 This drawing illustrates a brief sketch of a person making a long jump. Let's use this progression

to reach the symbol, 戉, that can be used to signify "to jump over."

As we learned earlier, 走 zǒu means "to walk." Putting 走 and 戉 together, the character, 越, signifies "stretching out two legs to walk then jump over." 越 yuè means "to jump over." One of the extended meanings of 越 is "more."

云越黑风越大，就越快下雨！
(雲越黑風越大，就越快下雨！)
yún yuè hēi fēng yuè dà   jiù yuè kuài xià yǔ
The blacker the cloud and the stronger the wind, the sooner it

starts to rain.

雨越来越大，他也越走越快！
(雨越來越大，他也越走越快！)
yǔ yuè lái yuè dà   tā yě yuè zǒu yuè kuài
The heavier the rain fell, the quicker he walked.

你越说他，他越不好好走路！
(你越說他，他越不好好走路！)
nǐ yuè shuō tā   tā yuè bú hǎo hǎo zǒu lù
The more you criticized him, the worse he walked!

朋友越多越开心！(朋友越多越開心！)
péng yǒu yuè duō yuè kāi xīn
The more friends we have, the happier we are!

他越说我越火！(他越說我越火！)
tā yuè shuō wǒ yuè huǒ
The more he says, the angrier I am!

她与我越来越好了。(她與我越來越好了。)
tā yǔ wǒ yuè lái yuè hǎo le
The relationship between her and me are getting better and
better.

You have learned:
...太阳藏在乌云后面，风开始用力吹，风刮的
越猛烈，行人越是
... fēng guā de yuè měng liè，xíng rén yuè shì

猛烈 měng liè
fierce

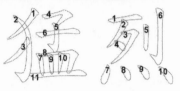

How do we express "fierce" in Chinese?

If we break apart the character 猛, it contains two parts: 犭 and 孟.

This drawing shows a sketch of a sitting dog.

Let's use this progression 犭 → 𠂇 → 犭
to reach the symbol, 犭. Usually, 犭 is used as a component of a character, which signifies that this character is related to a dog or "a kind of animal that looks like 犭 while sitting."

This drawing shows a sketch of an alert dog.

Let's use the progression

→ → → → 孟

to reach the character, 孟 mèng, which can be used to signify "a healthy or strong dog" and we can use 孟 to signify "violent" here.

孟子 mèng zǐ means "Mencius."

By putting 犭 and 孟 together, 猛 měng means

"fierce" or "vigorous."

Now let's look at the character, 烈.
If we break apart the character 烈, it contains
three parts: 歹, 刂, and 灬.
Let's examine the meaning of each part.

As we learned earlier, 歹 dǎi, means "evil" or
"bad." As we learned earlier, 刀 dāo means
"knife."
刂 is used as a radical for "knife."

灬 This is a radical for "fire." We can use 灬
to signify "ashes."

By putting 歹, 刂, and 灬 together, the
character, 烈, signifies "fierce with
dismembered body parts in ashes"; so, the
character, 烈 liè, is used to mean "fierce,"
"intense," or "violent."

* The liè sound is onomatopoeia. We may hear the liè sound
  if we listen to a very fierce fire.

烈日 liè rì means "scorching sun."
烈士 liè shì means "hero who died for the country" or "martyr."
烈女 liè nǚ means "a woman martyr," "a married woman who
commits suicide after the death of her husband or who dies in

defense of her honor."

猛烈 měng liè means "fierce."

风吹倒了树。(風吹倒了樹。)
fēng chuī dǎo le shù   Winds brought trees down.

大风吹倒了树。(大風吹倒了樹。)
dà fēng chuī dǎo le shù   Strong winds brought trees down.

猛烈的风吹倒了大树。(猛烈的風吹倒了大樹。)
měng liè de fēng chuī dǎo le dà shù
Fierce winds knocked down huge trees.

猛火 měng huǒ can be used to mean "raging fire."

猛士 měng shì means "brave soldier" or "brave person."

You have learned:

风与太阳正在争论谁的力量大。这时，他们看
到一个行人走在路上，太阳说："谁能使行人脱
下衣服，谁就力量大。"太阳藏在乌云后面，
风开始用力吹，风刮的越猛烈，行人越是

zhè shí，tā men kàn dào yī gè xíng rén zǒu zài lù
shàng，tài yáng shuō："shuí néng shǐ xíng rén tuō xià
yī fú shuí jiù lì liàng dà。"tài yáng cáng zài wū yún hòu
miàn，fēng kāi shǐ yòng lì chuī，fēng guā de yuè měng
liè，xíng rén yuè shì

是
shì
is; am; are; yes; was; were

是不是 shì bú shì means "whether or not."

问:是不是你说的？ 答:是我说的。答:不是我说的。
(問:是不是你說的？ 答:是我說的。答:不是我說的。)
wèn : shì bú shì nǐ shuō de   dá : shì wǒ shuō de
dá :   bú shì wǒ shuō de
Question: Whether you said it or not? Answer: I said it.
Answer: I didn't say it.

问:你是不是看到一只熊? 答:是，我看到一只熊！.
(問:你是不是看到一隻熊? 答:是，我看到一隻熊！)
wèn : nǐ shì bú shì kàn dào yī zhī xióng
dá : shì wǒ kàn dào yī zhī xióng
Q: Did you see a bear? A: Yes, I saw a bear.

问:是不是下雨了? 答:下雨了
wèn : shì bú shì xià yǔ le? dá : xià yǔ le
Q: Is it raining? A: Yes, it's raining.

问: 他是不是走了? 答: 他走了。
wèn : tā shì bú shì zǒu le？ dá : tā zǒu le。
Q: Has he left? A: Yes, he left.

这就是你的不是了。(這就是你的不是了。)
zhè jiù shì nǐ de bú shì le   This is your mistake.

你就是口太快了！
nǐ jiù shì kǒu tài kuài le
You are thoughtless in speech.

他们二人正在争论谁自私，是不是？

(他們二人正在爭論誰自私，是不是？)

tā men liǎng rén zhèng zài zhēng lùn shuí zì sī　shì bú shì

They two people are arguing about who is selfish, aren't they?

我问他，他们二人正在争论什么？他就是不说。

(我問他，他們二人正在爭論什麼？他就是不說。)

wǒ wèn tā　tā men liǎng rén zhèng zài zhēng lùn shí me
tā jiù shì bù shuō　I asked whether they two people were
arguing about something. But he just didn't want to say anything.

我问他们二人是不是好朋友？她就是不说。

(我問他們二人是不是好朋友？她就是不說。)

wǒ wèn tā men liǎng rén shì bú shì hǎo péng yǒu　tā jiù
shì bù shuō　I asked whether they two people are good friends.
But he just didn't want to say anything.

他是不是个自私的人？

(他是不是個自私的人？)

tā shì bú shì gè zì sī de rén　Is he a selfish person?

他躲在树上，是不是看到什么了？

(他躲在樹上，是不是看到什麼了？)

tā duǒ zài shù shàng　shì bú shì kàn dào shí me le

He is hiding in the tree, what has he seen?

他女朋友是不是来看他了？

(他女朋友是不是來看他了？)

tā nǚ péng yǒu shì bú shì lái kàn tā le

Has his girl friend come to see him?

抓 zhuā
to grasp

How do we construct a character that means "to grasp" in Chinese? Let's look at an animal's footprint first.

This drawing shows a sketch of an animal's footprint.

Let's use the progression 爪 ➞ 爪
to reach the character, 爪 zhuǎ, that is used as a general name for an animal's claw, talon, or paw. 熊爪 xióng zhǎo means "bear's paw."

This drawing shows a sketch of a hand.

Let's use the progression 扌 ➞ 扌 ➞ 扌
to reach the symbol, 扌, which is a radical for "hand."

By putting 扌 an 爪 together, 抓 signifies "using one's hand to grasp," so the character, 抓 zhuā, means "to grasp."

他们抓了一个人。(他們抓了一個人。)
tā men zhuā le yī gè rén
They caught a person.

紧紧 jǐn
tight

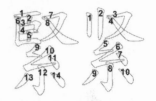

How do we construct a character that means "tight" in Chinese?

 These photos illustrate a person firmly gripping the rope. Let us use the character, 臣, to signify "the eye(◁) watching the rope while the person gripped the rope."

This can be used to signify "the rope."

Let's use the progression

to reach the character, 紧(緊) jǐn, that conveys the concept, "tight," "close," "urgent," or "strict."

抓紧(抓緊) zhuā jǐn means "to grip (something) tight."

风太大，我抓紧了衣服。

(風太大，我抓緊了衣服。)

fēng tài dà wǒ zhuā jǐn le yī fú

The wind was too strong, so I gripped my clothes tight!

人们抓到一只大熊。(人們抓到一隻大熊。)

rén men zhuā dào yī zhī dà xióng

People caught a big bear.

我们就要出发了，大家要抓紧时间。
(我們就要出發了，大家要抓緊時間。)

wǒ men jiù yào chū fā le dà jiā yào zhuā jǐn shí jiān

We are about to go, so we all should hurry up.

抓紧时间(抓緊時間) means "to hurry up."

The character, 要 yào/yāo, conveys the concept, "to ask for."

We will leran the character, 要, in the book, the Fox and The Goat. Here, 就要 conveys the concept, "about to."

The character, 发(發) fā, conveys the concept, "to send out."

We will leran the character, 发(發), in the book, the Fox and The Goat. Here, 出发(出發) means "to start a journey."

The character, 家 jiā, means "family." We will leran the character, 家, in Level 2 book. Here, 大家 means "we all."

The character, 间(間) shí jiān, conveys the concept, "between." We will leran the character, 时间(時間), in Level 2 book. Here, 时间(時間) means "time."

You have learned:

...风刮的越猛烈，行人越是抓紧

...fēng guā de yuè měng liè，xíng rén yuè shì zhuā jǐn

自己 zì jǐ
self

How do we construct the characters that mean "self" in Chinese? Let's look at our nose first!

Often Chinese people point to their own noses when saying "*myself*." The drawing, ㄥ or 𝐀, is a sketch of the nose from 2 different angles. By putting ㄥ on top of 𝐀, we get 𝐀.

Let's use the progression

ㄥ + 𝐀 → 𝐀 → 自 → 自

to reach the symbol, 自 zì, that could be used to mean "self."

我们喝开水，不能喝自来水。
（我們喝開水，不能喝自來水。）

wǒ men hē kāi shuǐ bù néng hē zì lái shuǐ

We drink boiled water. We shouldn't drink 自來水.

自來水 zì lái shuǐ means "water from the tap."

The character, 喝 means "to drink." The character, 喝, is well explained in the story, the Fox and The Goat.

不自在 bú zì zài means "not feel comfortable."

她一看到大熊就不自在。

tā yī kàn dào dà xióng jiù bú zì zài

She feels uncomfortable as soon as she sees the person called Da Xiong.

私自 sī zì conveys the concept, "alone," "secretly," or "without proper authorization." (自私 means "selfish.")

⟩ This is a brief sketch of a person's belly.

Let's use the progression

⟩ → ⟨ → 己 → 己 → 己

to reach the character, 己 jǐ, which also can be used to mean "self."

自己 zì jǐ is used to mean "self."

The chracters (自, 己, and 自己) all can be used to mean "self" in Chinese, but these characters are used in different contexts. **Generally, learners will understand the distinction as they read and use more Chinese.**

You have learned:

... 风刮的越猛烈，行人越是抓紧自己的

... fēng guā de yuè měng liè，xíng rén yuè shì zhuā jǐn zì jǐ de

出　chū
to exit

How do we construct a character that means "to exit" in Chinese?

⊻　This drawing signifies a plant sprouting upward out of the ground.

Let's use the progression

⊻→出→出

to reach the character, 出 chū, which is used to mean "to exit" in Chinese.

你说他是个自私的人，这我说不出口。

(你說他是個自私的人，這我說不出口。)

nǐ shuō tā shì gè zì sī de rén zhè wǒ shuō bù chū kǒu
You said he is a selfish person. I can't say this.
(Note: It's another way to say: I don't agree with you, I think he is not selfish, or I don't have proof for it.)

出口 chū kǒu means "to export," "exit," or "to speak."

他出门了！(他出門了！) tā chū mén le means "He goes out."

出来！ chū lái means "Come out!."

(A police may say 出来！ loudly to a thief in a house.)

熊来了，他躲到了树上，熊走了，他出来了。
(熊來了，他躲到了樹上，熊走了，他出來了。)
xióng lái le   tā duǒ dào le shù shàng   xióng zǒu le   tā chū lái le
As soon as the bear came, he hid in the tree; after the bear left,
he came out from hiding.

黑云走了，太阳出来了，太好了！
(黑雲走了，太陽出來了，太好了！)
hēi yún zǒu le   tài yáng chū lái le   tài hǎo le
So good the black cloud left and the sun comes out.

云开日出，我好开心！
(雲開日出，我好開心！)
yún kāi rì chū   wǒ hǎo kāi xīn
The sun comes out from behind the cloud! I am so happy!

日出 rì chū means "sunrise."

我看的出来，他好开心！
(我看的出來，他好開心！)
wǒ kàn de chū lái   tā hǎo kāi xīn
I can appreciate that he is so happy!

他自黑森林逃了出来。
(他自黑森林逃了出來。)
tā zì hēi sēn lín táo le chū lái
He escaped from the dark forest.

You have learned:
...太阳藏在乌云后面，风开始用力吹，风刮的
越猛烈，行人越是抓紧自己的衣服。太阳出
... tài yáng chū

來 来 lái
to come

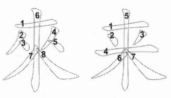

出来(出來) chū lái means "to come out."

你出来！(你出來！) nǐ chū lái means "You, come out!"

你下来！(你下來！) nǐ xià lái means "You, come down!"

上来(上來)！ shàng lái means "Come up!"

来！(來!) lái means "Come!"

来！来！(來! 來!) lái lái means "Come! Come!"

你来不来？(你來不來？) nǐ lái bù lái means "Will you come?"

一来..., 二来..., 三来... (一來..., 二來..., 三來...)
yī lái èr lái sān lái means "Firstly..., secondly..., thirdly...."

他来了！(他來了！) tā lái le means "He has come!"

他来看你了！(他來看你了！) tā lái kàn nǐ le
means "He has come to see you!"

后来，熊也爬上了树！(後來，熊也爬上了樹！)
hòu lái   xióng yě pá shàng le shù
Later on, the bear also climbed into the tree.

刮大风又下大雨，看来他不能来了！
(刮大風又下大雨，看來他不能來了！)
guā dà fēng yòu xià dà yǔ   kàn lái tā bù néng lái le
It seems like he can't come because of strong wind and heavy rain.
You have learned: 太阳出来

了 le
A function character to
indicate a past tense

 太阳出来了！(太陽出來了！)
tài yáng chū lái le   The sun has come out.

后来，他来了。(後來，他來了。)
hòu lái   tā lái le   Later on, he came!

我来，是为了看日出。(我來，是為了看日出。)
wǒ lái shì wéi le kàn rì chū
I come (here) in order to see sunrise.

他不来了。(他不來了。)
tā bù lái le   He will not come.

他走不了！tā zǒu bù liǎo means "I am unable to leave."

没什么大不了的！(沒什麼大不了的！)
méi shí me dà bù le de
It's nothing frightening. It's nothing to worry about.

后来，熊逃走了！(後來，熊逃走了！)
hòu lái   xióng táo zǒu le   The bear has escaped.

他快到了！tā kuài dào le He shall arrive soon.

他火了！ tā huǒ le   He became angry!

You have learned:
...太阳出来了   tài yáng chū lái le
... the sun came out

nuǎn
warm

How do we construct a character that means "warm" in Chinese?

If we break apart the character 爰, it contains three parts: ⺈, 干, and 又.
Let's find out the meaning of each part.

This drawing could be used to signify a sketch of a hand.
Let's use the progression

to reach the symbol, ⺈, which can be used to signify "hand."

干 This drawing shows a device that both parties can hold onto when one is rescuing the other.

Let's use the progression

to reach the symbol, 又, which also can be used to signify a "hand."

By putting ⺈, 干, and 又 together, 爰 can be

used to signify "one helping another."

☼ This drawing shows a sketch of the sun. If we look at the sun through a pair of very dark sunglasses, the sun looks like ⊙.

Let's use the progression
⊙ → ⊖ → 日 → 日
to reach the character, 日 rì, that means "sun" in Chinese.

By putting 日 and 爰 together, the character 暖 signifies "the sun is sending out heat," so the character, 暖 nuǎn, means "warm" in Chinese.

The word, 暖暖 nuǎn nuǎn, still means "warm," though 暖暖 is more often used orally.

暖风(暖風) nuǎn fēng means "genial breezes."
暖暖的阳光(暖暖的陽光) nuǎn nuǎn de yáng guāng means "warm sunshine."
暖暖的大手 nuǎn nuǎn de dà shǒu means "a warm big hand."

You have learned:
太阳藏在乌云后面，风开始用力吹，风刮的越猛烈，行人越是抓紧自己的衣服。太阳出来了，暖暖的
... tài yáng chū lái le   nuǎn nuǎn de

照 zhào
to Illuminate; to shine on

How do we construct a character that means "to illuminate" in Chinese?

 This illustrates "sun over the salt pan."

Let's use the progression

to reach the character, 照 zhào, that is used to mean "to shine on" or "to illuminate."

日照 rì zhào means "sunshine."

夕照 xī zhào means "glow of sunset" or "the reflected light of sunset."

太阳照向行人，行人热了。
(太陽照向行人，行人熱了。)
tài yáng zhào xiàng xíng rén　xíng rén rè le
The Sun shone warmly upon the man, then he fell hot.

You have learned:
... 太阳出来了，暖暖的照
... tài yáng chū lái le nuǎn nuǎn de zhào

向 xiàng
direction; towards

How do we construct a character that means "direction" in Chinese?

Generally, Chinese people prefer to live in a south-facing house. For ancient Chinese houses, by looking at the window of a house you may get to know the direction.

⋂ This shows a sketch of a house.

▯ This can be used to signify a window.

By putting the house ⋂ and ▯ together, 向 is used to signify "direction." So, the character, 向 xiàng, means "direction." One of the extended meanings of 向 is "towards."

熊是不是一向不吃死人？
xióng shì bú shì yī xiàng bù chī sǐ rén
Is bear used not to eat dead people?

一向 yī xiàng means "always" or "used to."

熊向你说了什么？(熊向你說了什麼？)
xióng xiàng nǐ shuō le shí me
What did the bear say to you?

向来(向來) xiàng lái means "usually, in the past."

向后一看，他看到一只熊。

(向後一看，他看到一隻熊。)

xiàng hòu yī kàn　tā kàn dào yī zhī xióng

After looking backwards, he saw a bear.

向后(向後) means "backward."

看了看云与风向，他说：快下雨了！

(看了看雲與風向，他說：快下雨了！)

kàn le kàn yún yǔ fēng xiàng　tā shuō　kuài xià yǔ le

After looking at cloud and the direction of the wind, he said: it is going to rain soon!

向上看 xiàng shàng kàn means "looking upwards."

向下看 xiàng xià kàn means "looking downwards."

爬上了树，他向下看，看到熊在他朋友的脸上闻了闻，就走了。(爬上了樹，他向下看，看到熊在他朋友的臉上聞了聞，就走了。)

pá shàng le shù　tā xiàng xià kàn　kàn dào xióng zài tā péng yǒu de liǎn shàng wén le wén　jiù zǒu le

After climbing into the tree, he looked downwards and saw the bear put its nose to his friend's face, and sniffed briefly, then the bear went away.

向心力 xiàng xīn lì means "centripetal force."

向阳的树(向陽的樹) xiàng yáng de shù means "the trees facing the sun."

You have learned:

...太阳出来了，暖暖的照向

... tài yáng chū lái le　nuǎn nuǎn de zhào xiàng

熱 热 rè
hot

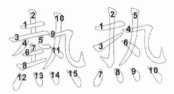

How do we construct a character that means "hot" in Chinese?

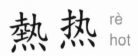 This drawing shows a sketch of a fire. Let's use this progression

𤆍 ➝ 火 ➝ 火

to reach the character, 火 huǒ, which means "fire."

This picture illustrates that a person is adding firewood to the fire. At that moment, he felt **_hot_**.

Let's use the progression

to reach the symbol, 热(熱) rè, that signifies "It's a big fire, even the ground is hot with the ash, and the person is facing the heat." The character, 热(熱)rè, means "hot." The symbol, 丸, looks like the person adding firewood to

the fire, ![radical]. (The radical 扌 signifies a hand.)
•••• This can be used to signify the "burning ashes" from the big fire.

她是个热心的人，她是我的好朋友。
(她是個熱心的人，她是我的好朋友。)
tā shì gè rè xīn de rén tā shì wǒ de hǎo péng yǒu
She is a warm-hearted person. She is my good friend.

在大太阳下走路，好热！
(在大太陽下走路，好熱！)
zài dà tài yáng xià zǒu lù hǎo rè
Walking under the strong sun, it's very hot.

太热了，他不出门。(太熱了，他不出門。)
tài rè le tā bù chū mén
It is too hot. He doesn't go out.

好热，我热死了！(好熱，我熱死了！)
hǎo rè　wǒ rè sǐ le　So hot! It is unbearabe.
热死(熱死) rè sǐ means "unbearably hot" or "to die of sunstroke."

热水(熱水) rè shuǐ means "hot water."
热开水(熱開水) rè kāi shuǐ means "hot boiled water."
开水(開水) kāi shuǐ means "boiled water."

You have learned:
太阳出来了，暖暖的照向行人，行人热了，
... The passenger felt hot.

很　hěn
very

How do we construct a character to express "very" in Chinese?

 This picture illustrates **two people** were looking and talking about a **very** different **tree root**.

Let's use the progression

很 → 仴艮 → 佷 → 很 → 很

to reach the character, the character, 很 hěn, means "very."

这只黑熊的力量很大。
(這隻黑熊的力量很大。)
zhè zhī hēi xióng de lì liàng hěn dà
The black bear is very powerful.

You have learned:
风与太阳正在争论谁的力量大。
这时，他们看到一个行人走在路上，太阳说："
谁能使行人脱下衣服，谁就力量大。"
太阳藏在乌云后面，风开始用力吹，风刮的越
猛烈，行人越是抓紧自己的衣服。 太阳出来了，
暖暖的照向行人，行人热了，很

快

kuài
quick

这一个行人走的很快。
(這一個行人走的很快。)
zhè yī gè xíng rén zǒu de hěn kuài。
This pedestrian is walking very fast.

一看到熊，他很快就爬上了树。
(一看到熊，他很快就爬上了樹。)
yī kàn dào xióng tā hěn kuài jiù pá shàng le shù
He climbed into the tree, as soon as he saw the bear.

你一到，她很快就看到你了。
nǐ yī dào tā hěn kuài jiù kàn dào nǐ le
She saw you quickly as soon as you arrived.

快！快开门！(快！快開門！)
kuài kuài kāi mén   Quick! Open the door quickly!

水快开了！(水快開了！)
shuǐ kuài kāi le   The water is about boiling.

You have learned:
太阳藏在乌云后面，风开始用力吹，风刮的越
猛烈，行人越是抓紧自己的衣服。太阳出来了，
暖暖的照向行人，行人热了，很快
... tài yáng chū lái le，nuǎn nuǎn de zhào xiàng xíng
rén，xíng rén rè le，hěn kuài

把  bǎ
to hold

How do we construct a character that means "to hold" in Chinese?

 This sketch shows a parent holding and helping a baby to pee. Lots of Chinese parents did this when their baby was very little.

𝅘 This drawing shows a sketch of a hand. Let's use the progression

𝔍 → 扌 → 扌

to reach the symbol, 扌 , which signifies "a hand" and 扌 is a redical for "hand."

𝆏 This can be further modified as 扑.

巴 or 巴 This looks like the sketch of the baby 𝆏.

Let's use the progression

𝆏 → 扑 → 把 → 把

to reach the character, 把 bǎ, that signifies "to hold" or "the parent is handling the situation";

so,把 bǎ is used to mean "to hold" or "to grasp" in Chinese. When 把 is pronounced bà, 把 means "a handle" in Chinese.

一把刀 yī bǎ dāo means "a knife."

把 bǎ is also a measure word.

一把筷子 yī bǎ kuài zǐ means "a handful of chopsticks."

一把竹筷子 yī bǎ zhú kuài zǐ means "a handful of bamboo chopsticks."

一把 yī bǎ means "a handful of."

一大把 yī dà bǎ means "a full handful of."

火把 huǒ bǎ means "fire torch."

刀把子 dāo bà zǐ means "a knife handle."

他是个把风的。(他是個把風的。)
tā shì gè bǎ fēng de   He is a lookout.

把风(把風) bǎ fēng means "be on the lookout (of thieves' colleague)."

大风把树吹倒了。(大風把樹吹倒了。)
dà fēng bǎ shù chuī dǎo le
The tree was blown down by strong wind.

巴 or 巴 This also shows a sketch of a rock climbing person, 🧗.

Let's use the progression 🚶 → 卩 → 巴
to reach the character, 巴 bā, which means "to stick to" in Chinese, just as the rock climber must stick to the rock face.

下巴 xià bā means "chin."

巴士 bā shì means "bus."
The English word, bus, has been phonetically translated into Chinese as 巴士 bā shì. In other words, the word 巴士 is a phonetically imported word from the English word, bus.

大巴士 dà bā shì means "big bus."

他上了巴士，走了。
tā shàng le bā shì   zǒu le
He got on a bus and left.

You have learned:

风与太阳正在争论谁的力量大。这时，他们看到一个行人走在路上，太阳说："谁能使行人脱下衣服，谁就力量大。"太阳藏在乌云后面，风开始用力吹，风刮的越猛烈，行人越是抓紧自己的衣服。太阳出来了，暖暖的照向行人，行人热了，很快把

... tài yáng chū lái le，nuǎn nuǎn de zhào xiàng xíng rén，xíng rén rè le，hěn kuài bǎ
...Then the Sun came out and shone warmly upon the man. As the man walked, he found it was too hot. Quickly he took

外 wài
outside

How do we construct a character that means "outside" in Chinese?

If we break apart the character 外, it contains two parts: 夕 and 卜. Let's find out the meaning of each part.

We have learned the character, 卜 bǔ, means "divine" or "foretell" in Chinese.

The character, 夕, looks like a half moon or a new moon. 夕 xī can be used to signify "evening" or "night." 夕 also conveys the concept, "sunset," "evening," or "night."

By putting 夕 and 卜 together, 外 could be used to signify "*outside* of the turtle shell," since it was the outside that was used in fortune telling. The character, 外 wài, means "outside."

Earlier we learned that 衣 yī means "clothes" in Chinese. So, 外衣 wài yī means "outer clothing."

外耳 wài ěr means "external ear."

熊在门外。(熊在門外。)
xióng zài mén wài
The bear is outside the door.

谁在门外？(誰在門外？)
shuí zài mén wài
Who is it outside the door?

在门外的是谁？(在門外的是誰？)
zài mén wài de shì shuí
Who is it outside the door?

外面谁来了？(外面誰來了？)
wài miàn shuí lái le
Who is there outside the door?

中外人士 zhōng wài rén shì means "Chinese and foreigners."

You have learned:
...太阳出来了，暖暖的照向行人，行人热了，很快把外衣脱下。

... tài yáng chū lái le，nuǎn nuǎn de zhào xiàng xíng rén，xíng rén rè le，hěn kuài bǎ wài yī tuō xià。

... the Sun came out and shone warmly upon the man. As the man walked, he found it was too hot. Quickly he took off his outer clothing.

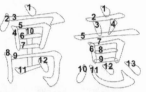

寓意 yù yì
implied meaning

How do we construct two characters that mean "implied meaning" in Chinese? Let's look at a monkey's sketch first!

This drawing shows a sketch of a mother monkey.

弓 or 止 This drawing shows a sketch of a baby monkey.

This drawing shows a sketch of a mother monkey with her baby.

Let's use this progression

👹 → 内 → 禺 → 禺

to reach the symbol, 禺, which signifies "the baby monkey stays with her mother while young" or "a temporary stay."

∩ or ⌂ This shows a simple sketch of a house. By putting ⌂ and 禺 together, 寓 or 寓 signifies "a monkey with her baby that stays in a house."

Try to think of it like this: If you saw a monkey with her baby in a house, you might think it has all the makings of a fairy tale or a story passed down from generations. So, 寓 yù is used to mean "sojourn," "to imply," or "fable."

How do we construct a character to express "implied meaning" in Chinese? Let's look at a sketch of a gong first!

This shows a sketch of a gong.

Let's use the progression

回 → 𠮷 → 音 → 音

to reach the character, 音 yīn, that means "sound," because a gong was a loud and important instrument in ancient China.

By putting 音 and 心 together, 意 signifies "the sound of mind" or "meaning." Therefore, the character, 意 yì, represents "meaning."

By putting 寓 and 意 together, the word, 寓意 yù yì, means "implied meaning," "deeper meaning," or "moral of the story."

子音 zǐ yīn means "(phonetics) consonants."

意外 yì wài means "accident."

你这么说，用意是什么？
(你這麼說，用意是什麼？)
nǐ zhè me shuō   yòng yì shì shí me
What's yout intention for what you said?
用意 means "intention, careful thought or hidden purpose."

你这么说，我不在意。(你這麼說，我不在意。)
nǐ zhè me shuō   wǒ bú zài yì
I don't care you said this this way.
不在意 bú zài yì means "not concerned."

你说什么，我不在意。(你說什麼，我不在意。)
nǐ shuō shí me   wǒ bú zài yì
What's your intention for what you said?

我在意你说什么。(我在意你說什麼)
wǒ zài yì nǐ shuō shí me
I care about what you said.
在意 zài yì means "care about."

You have learned:
... 太阳出来了，暖暖的照向行人，行人热了，
很快把外衣脱下。寓意：
... tài yáng chū lái le，nuǎn nuǎn de zhào xiàng xíng
rén，xíng rén rè le，hěn kuài bǎ wài yī tuō xià。yù yì
... the Sun came out and shone warmly upon the man.
As the man walked, he found it was too hot. Quickly
he took off his outer clothing. Implied meaning:

溫 温　wēn
　　　gentle; warm

How do we construct a character that means "gentle" in Chinese?

Traditionally, Chinese had a special way to warm up certain kinds of alcohol just before drinking it.

 This shows a sketch of how Chinese warm up the alcohol.

Let's use the progression

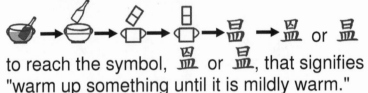

to reach the symbol, 显 or 显, that signifies "warm up something until it is mildly warm."

Now we will find out what 氵 stands for.

≋ This shows a sketch of a river. We can feel the running water in the river.

Let's use the progression ≋ → ⋮ → 氵

to reach the symbol, 氵, that is usually an indication of liquid or water. When 氵 is used as a component of other characters, these characters are usually associated with water or liquid.

Let's use the progression 川 → 川 → 水 to reach the character, 水 shuǐ, that means "water" in Chinese.

Now, by putting 氵 and 昷 together, 温(溫) wēn means "warm" in Chinese. One of the extended meanings of 温(溫) is "gentle."

温水(溫水) wēn shuǐ means "warm water."

水温(水溫) shuǐ wēn means "the temperature of the water."

温热的水(溫熱的水) wēn rè de shuǐ means "warm to hot water."

温暖的手(溫暖的手) wēn nuǎn de shǒu means "warm hand."

You have learned:

风与太阳正在争论谁的力量大。

这时，他们看到一个行人走在路上，太阳说："谁能使行人脱下衣服，谁就力量大。"

太阳藏在乌云后面，风开始用力吹，风刮的越猛烈，行人越是抓紧自己的衣服。

太阳出来了，暖暖的照向行人，行人热了，很快把外衣脱下。寓意：温

和 hé
peace; harmony; harmonious

How do we construct a character that means "peace" in Chinese? Let's take a look at a "sheng" first!

This is a wind instrument called "sheng."
Each sheng contains a number of pipes,
with a blowhole on the bottom of the
instrument.

Let's use the progression

to reach the character, 和, that was used to
signify "peace," "harmony," or "harmonious,"
because ancient Chinese thought the sound
of this instrument is harmonious. The
character, 和 hé, means "peace," "harmony,"
"harmonious," or "and."

我和他是好朋友。
wǒ hé tā shì hǎo péng yǒu
He and I are good friends.
我和他是好朋友 is more colloquial than 我与他是
好朋友(我與他是好朋友).

常 cháng
often

How do we construct a Chinese character to express "often?" Let's look at a towel first!

 This photo shows a towel.

Let's use the progression

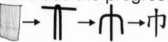

to reach the character, 巾 jīn, that means "towel."

手巾 shǒu jīn means "a handkerchief."

面巾 miàn jīn means "face towel."

In ancient China, many people wore two pieces of clothing, an upper part (a shirt) and a lower part (a wrap-around skirt.)

 This drawing can be used to signify a brief sketch of a skirt: the belt, the old style buckle, and the skirt.

Let's use the progression

to reach the character, 常 cháng, which is used to mean "often" because it was the clothing most commonly wore by people in ancient China. 常常 cháng cháng still means often, though 常常 is more often used orally.

他常来看我。(他常來看我。)
tā cháng lái kàn wǒ   He often comes to visit me.

他常说我是他的好朋友。
(他常說我是他的好朋友。)
tā cháng shuō wǒ shì tā de hǎo péng yǒu
He often says that I am his good friend.

他常和人们争论。(他常和人們爭論。)
tā cháng hé rén men zhēng lùn
He often argues with others.

"风与太阳"是个寓言。("風與太陽"是個寓言。)
fēng yǔ tài yáng shì gè yù yán
"The Wind and The Sun" is a fable.

You have learned:
... 太阳出来了，暖暖的照向行人，行人热了，很快把外衣脱下。
寓意：温和的力量常常
... tài yáng chū lái le，nuǎn nuǎn de zhào xiàng xíng rén，xíng rén rè le，hěn kuài bǎ wài yī tuō xià。
yù yì : wēn hé de lì liàng cháng cháng gèng

更 gèng
more; to change

How do we construct a character that means "more" in Chinese? Let's look at an old Chinese tradition first!

In ancient China, most people went to bed early and got up early. At night, security guard walked through the streets with a piece of wood and a gong. After banging on the gong while on patrol, the guards would yell out announcements like the time, or warnings, e.g. "It's 3am! Be careful about fire or thieves." So people felt the *change* of the time at night.

At 7pm, the guard would hit the wood and the gong once. At 9pm, the guard hit the wood twice and the gong once. At 11pm, the guard hit the wood three times and the gong once. So, as the time went by at night, people heard *more* sound from the hitting of the wood.

The patrol started at 7pm and ended at 3am, which was the time for ancient Chinese to get up or even the emperor to get up to prepare for his palace meeting at 5am.

This drawing shows an illustration to describe the scene.
This drawing is the abstraction of the scene, because most people only notice the gong and its sound."

Let's use the progression ⛿ → ⛿ → 更

to reach the character, 更 gèng, which means "to change" or "more" in Chinese. The drawing, 乂, signifies "a hand."

更多的人来看你了！(更多的人來看你了！)
gèng duō de rén lái kàn nǐ le
More people are here to visit you.

你走的快，他走的更快！
nǐ zǒu de kuài   tā zǒu de gèng kuài
You walk fast enough. He walks even faster.

你爬树爬的快，熊爬树爬的更快！
(你爬樹爬的快，熊爬樹爬的更快！)
nǐ pá shù pá de kuài   xióng pá shù pá de gèng kuài
You climb trees fast enough. The bear climbs trees even faster.

看到熊，你逃的快，他逃的更快！
kàn dào xióng   nǐ táo de kuài   tā táo de gèng kuài
After seeing a bear, you fled away fast, but he fled away even faster.

熊来了，你躲的快，他藏的更快！
(熊來了，你躲的快，他藏的更快！)

xióng lái le　nǐ duǒ de kuài　tā cáng de gèng kuài
If a bear came, you would go hiding fast and he would go hiding even faster.

他自私，他的朋友更自私！
tā zì sī　tā de péng yǒu gèng zì sī
He was selfish, but his friend was even more selfish.

你的力量大，熊的力量更大！
nǐ de lì liàng dà　xióng de lì liàng gèng dà
You are powerful, but the bear is even more powerful.

你说的快，他说的更快！
(你說的快，他說的更快！)
nǐ shuō de kuài　tā shuō de gèng kuài
You speak fast, but he speaks even faster.

三更 sān gēng means "midnight" or "time between 11pm and 1am."

更衣 gèng yī means "to change dress."

我们快出门了，她正在更衣。
(我們快出門了，她正在更衣。)
wǒ men kuài chū mén le　tā zhèng zài gèng yī
We are going to leave. He is changing his clothes.

You have learned:
... 太阳出来了，暖暖的照向行人，行人热了，很快把外衣脱下。寓意：温和的力量常常更
... yù yì : wēn hé de lì liàng cháng cháng gèng
... Implied meaning: Being peaceful is often a more

為 为
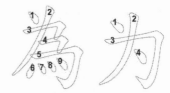

wéi   to do; to be
wèi   on account of

How do we construct a character to express "on account of" in Chinese?

 This sketch shows "a person is riding on an elephant and the elephant is doing some kind of work." As a person watches the scene, a question may come up in his mind: "**What** are they **do**ing?"

Let's use the progression

to reach the character, 为(為), that signifies "to do (something)" or "is." 为(為) wéi means "to do" or "to be." The usuage of 为(為) wèi is similar to "on account of."

更为(更為) gèng wéi conveys the concept, "more."

你为什么常和人们争论？
(你為什麼常和人們爭論？)
nǐ wèi shí me cháng hé rén men zhēng lùn
Why do you argue with others so often?
为什么(為什麼) wèi shí me means "why."

你为什么不快逃？（你為什麼不快逃？）
nǐ wèi shí me bú kuài táo
Why didn't you run away quickly?

你为什么不能立刻来看我？
（你為什麼不能立刻來看我？）
nǐ wèi shí me bù néng lì kè lái kàn wǒ
Why can't you come to see me immediately?

看到熊来了，你为什么不快逃走？
（看到熊來了，你為什麼不快逃走？）
kàn dào xióng lái le nǐ wèi shí me bú kuài táo zǒu
Why didn't you run away quickly, after you saw the bear came?

为什么水这么热？（為什麼水這麼熱？）
wèi shí me shuǐ zhè me rè
Why is the water so hot?

我问她为什么。（我問她為什麼。）
wǒ wèn tā wèi shí me　I asked her why.

我问她，为什么常和人们争论？
（我問她，為什麼常和人們爭論？）
wǒ wèn tā wèi shí me cháng hé rén men zhēng lùn
I asked her why she argued with others so often.

我问她，为什么不快逃？
（我問她，為什麼不快逃？）
wǒ wèn tā wèi shí me bú kuài táo
I asked her why she didn't run away quickly.

我问她，为什么不能立刻来看我？
(我問她，為什麼不能立刻來看我？)
wǒ wèn tā wèi shí me bù néng lì kè lái kàn wǒ
I asked her why she couldn't come to see me immediately?

我问她，为什么看到熊来了，不快逃走？
(我問她，為什麼看到熊來了，不快逃走？)
wǒ wèn tā wèi shí me kàn dào xióng lái le bú kuài táo zǒu
I asked her why she didn't run away quickly, after she saw the
bear coming.

我问她为什么水这么热？
(我問她為什麼水這麼熱？)
wǒ wèn tā wèi shí me shuǐ zhè me rè
I asked her why the water was so hot.

风与太阳为什么在争论？
(風與太陽為什麼在爭論？)
fēng yǔ tài yáng wéi shí me zài zhēng lùn
Why were wind and sun arguing?

风与太阳在争论什么？
(風與太陽在爭論什麼？)
fēng yǔ tài yáng zài zhēng lùn shí me
What were wind and sun arguing about?

行人为什么脱下衣服？
(行人為什麼脫下衣服？)
háng rén wéi shí me tuō xià yī fú
Why did the pedestrian take off his outer clothing?

有 yǒu
to possess; to have

How do we construct a character that means "to have" in Chinese? Let's look at the Chinese character 有 directly!

If we break apart the character 有, it contains two parts: 𠂇 and 月.
Let's find out the meaning of each part.

This drawing shows the sketch of a hand.

Let's use the progression ⇛ → ⋋ → 𠂇 to reach the symbol, 𠂇, which signifies a hand.

月 or 月 This looks like a chunk of pork hanging at a butcher's shop and it also looks like a moon. The moon goes around the earth monthly. So 月 ròu signifies "meat," "flesh," or "body," and 月 yuè means "moon" or "month."

It was common in ancient China for neighbors or friends to share things, such as meat, with others. For a visitor with a piece of meat in his hand, perhaps he may say, "I ***have*** the meat to share with you." So, by putting 宀 and 月 together,有 can be used to signify "I own this" or "I ***have*** the meat to share with you."

The character, 有 yǒu, is used to mean "to have" or "to possess."

我有一只熊、三只马。
(我有一隻熊、三隻馬。)
wǒ yǒu yī zhī xióng　sān zhī mǎ
I have 1 bear and 3 bears.

你是不是有把刀？　nǐ shì bú shì yǒu bǎ dāo
Do you have a knife?

森林中是不是有熊？
sēn lín zhōng shì bú shì yǒu xióng
Are there bears in the forest?

是不是有筷子？　shì bú shì yǒu kuài zǐ
Do you have chopsticks?
(You may say this sentence, when you enter a Chinese restaurant and try to get chopsticks there.)

You have learned:
... 太阳出来了，暖暖的照向行人，行人热了，
很快把外衣脱下。寓意：温和的力量常常更为
有 ... tài yáng chū lái le，nuǎn nuǎn de zhào xiàng
xíng rén，xíng rén rè le，hěn kuài bǎ wài yī tuō xià。
yù yì：wēn hé de lì liàng cháng cháng gèng wéi yǒu

效 xiào
effectiveness

How do we construct a character that means "effect" in Chinese? Let's look at how people presented gifts to an emperor first!

 This picture illustrates "a farmer presenting his best harvest to an Emperor." The picture can be used to signify "**hand in**."

Let's use the progression

$$\text{大} \rightarrow \text{大} \rightarrow \text{大} \rightarrow \text{交}$$

to reach the character, 交 jiāo, which means "to hand in."

A long time ago, when students didn't finish homework or didn't behave as expected, a few teachers may beat children with rattan canes.

 This drawing illustrates a hand holding a beating stick.

Let's use the progression

辶 → 辷 → 夊 → 夂 → 夂 → 夂

to reach the symbol, 夂, which can be used to signify "to ask for (better performance or effectiveness)."

By putting 交 and 夂 together, 效 signifies "ask for effectiveness"; 效 xiào is used to mean "effectiveness" or "to follow the example of."

Congratulations!

You have learned all characters in the story, and you should be able to read and understand the story completely in Chinese on the following page!

Title: 風與太陽(Traditional Chinese)

風與太陽正在爭論誰的力量大。

這時，他們看到一個行人走在路上，太陽說："
誰能使行人脫下衣服誰就力量大。"

太陽藏在烏雲後面，風開始用力吹，風刮的越
猛烈，行人越是抓緊自己的衣服。

太陽出來了，暖暖的照向行人，行人熱了，很
快把外衣脫下。

寓意：溫和的力量常常更為有效。

Characters also learned in the book:

蟲大寸固吏史鳥火黑兩卜刂舌列灬爪臣巴音水
巾交

Title: 风与太阳(Simplified Chinese)

风与太阳正在争论谁的力量大。

这时，他们看到一个行人走在路上，太阳说："
谁能使行人脱下衣服，谁就力量大。"

太阳藏在乌云后面，风开始用力吹，风刮的越
猛烈，行人越是抓紧自己的衣服。

太阳出来了，暖暖的照向行人，行人热了，很
快把外衣脱下。

寓意：温和的力量常常更为有效。

虫大寸固吏史鸟火黑兩卜刂舌列灬爪臣巴音水
巾交

fēng yǔ tài yáng zhèng zài zhēng lùn shuí de lì liàng dà。zhè shí, tā men kàn dào yī gè xíng rén zǒu zài lù shàng, tài yáng shuō : "shuí néng shǐ xíng rén tuō xià yī fú shuí jiù lì liàng dà。"

tài yáng cáng zài wū yún hòu miàn, fēng kāi shǐ yòng lì chuī, fēng guā de yuè měng liè, xíng rén yuè shì zhuā jǐn zì jǐ de yī fú。

tài yáng chū lái le, nuǎn nuǎn de zhào xiàng xíng rén, xíng rén rè le, hěn kuài bǎ wài yī tuō xià。

yù yì : wēn hé de lì liàng cháng cháng gèng wéi yǒu xiào。

The Wind and the Sun were arguing which one was more powerful. At this moment, they saw a pedestrian walking down the road, and the Sun said: "Whichever of us can cause him to take off his clothing shall be regarded as more powerful." So the Sun hid behind the dark cloud, and the Wind began to blow hard upon the man. However the harder the Wind blew, the tighter the man held on to his clothing. Then the Sun came out and shone warmly upon the man. As the man walked, he found it was too hot. Quickly he took off his outer clothing. Implied meaning: Being peaceful is often a more effective method.

We have learned some Chinese characters from two stories. Now we can try and make some simple sentences.

我们交个朋友！（我們交個朋友！）
wǒ men jiāo gè péng yǒu   Let's be friends!
交朋友 jiāo péng yǒu means "be friends."

人们不和自私的人交友！
（人們不和自私的人交友！）
rén men bú hé zì sī de rén jiāo yǒu
People don't make friends with selfish people.
Here, 交友 jiāo yǒu is short for 交朋友 jiāo péng yǒu.

你介意我用这把刀吗？
（你介意我用這把刀嗎？）
nǐ jiè yì wǒ yòng zhè bǎ dāo ma
Do you mind me using this knife?
Here, 介意 jiè yì means "to care about."
(We will learn the character, 吗(嗎), in the the story, The Fox and The Goat. 吗(嗎) indicates "a question mark.")

你说什么，我不在意！（你說什麼，我不在意！）
nǐ shuō shí me   wǒ bú zài yì
I don't mind what you said.

她是个中国人吗？（她是個中國人嗎？）
tā shì gè zhōng guó rén ma   Is she a Chinese?

(Ancient Chinese thought China was in the middle of the world.)

中国(中國) zhōng guó means "China." (We will learn the character, 国(國), in the Level 2 book. The character, 国 (國), guó means "country" or "nation.")

中立国(中立國) zhōng lì guó "neutral country."
中立 zhōng lì guó means "neutral."

交出你的刀子！jiāo chū nǐde dāo zǐ means "Surrander your kinfe!"

外交 wài jiāo means "diplomacy."

时装(時裝) shí zhuāng means "fashionable dress."

死水 sǐ shuǐ means "stagnant water."
好死 hǎo sǐ means "to die a natural death."

他是个能人。(他是個能人。)
tā shì gè néng rén   He is an able person.

他不来看她，她死心了！
(他不来看她，她死心了！)
tā bù lái kàn tā   tā sǐ xīn le
He didn't come to see her. She gave up her hope.
死心 to give up hope (of romance, etc.)

风闻他到国外了！(風聞他到國外了！)
fēng wén tā dào guó wài le   I heard he went overseas.
风闻(風聞) means "to hear by rumor or hear from gossip."

他在国外水土不服，一到中国就好了。
(他在國外水土不服，一到中國就好了。)

tā zài guó wài shuǐ tǔ bù fú yī dào zhōng guó jiù hǎo le
He was not well in overseas because he wasn't accustomed
himself to the climate or diet of this country, but he became well
as soon as he returned to China.

水土不服 means "not accustomed to the climate or diet of a
place."

Either 我走不了！wǒ zǒu bù liǎo or 我走不开！(我
走不開！) wǒ zǒu bù kāi means "I can't leave."

你走的好快！
nǐ zǒu de hǎo kuài   You walk so fast.

他在路上，马上到！(他在路上，馬上到！)
tā zài lù shàng mǎ shàng dào
He is on the way here. He will arrive very soon.

水路 shuǐ lù means "waterway."

口水 kǒu shuǐ means "saliva."

风衣(風衣) wǒ zǒu bù kāi means "coat , jacket, or
windbreaker designed for windy days".

树上有三只鸟。(樹上有三隻鳥。)
shù shàng yǒu sān zhī niǎo
There are 3 birds on the tree.

十个月后，32 日人来看她！
(十個月後，32 日人來看她！)
shí gè yuè hòu sān shí èr rì rén lái kàn tā

10 months later, 32 Japanese came to visit her.

十个月后，三十二日人来看她！

(十個月後，三十二日人來看她！)

shí gè yuè hòu sān shí èr rì rén lái kàn tā

10 months later, 32 Japanese came to visit her.

(This sentence is the same as last sentence.)

十月后，32 日人来中国看她！

(十月後，32 日人來中國看她！)

shí yuè hòu sān shí èr rì rén lái zhōng guó kàn tā

After October, 32 Japanese will come to visit her in China.

(This sentence also may mean: 10 months later, 32 Japanese came to visit her.)(After all, for the past several thousand years, most Chinese have lived in agricultural societies, so a lot of Chinese don't have the need to express themseves precisely in one sentence. Sometimes, we can get the exact meaning by reading more in the article.)

10 月 3 日，12 日人来中国看她！

(10 月 3 日，12 日人來中國看她！)

shí yuè sān rì   shí èr rì rén lái zhōng guó kàn tā

On October 3, 12 Japanese came to China to visit her.

10 月 3 日，12 日人来中国看她了！

(10 月 3 日，12 日人來中國看她了！)

shí yuè sān rì   shí èr rì rén lái zhōng guó kàn tā le

On October 3, 12 Japanese came to China to see her.

11 月 3 日，22 日人来中国看她了！

(11 月 3 日，22 日人來中國看她了！)

shí yī yuè sān rì   èr shí èr rì rén lái zhōng guó kàn tā le

On November 3, 22 Japanese came to China to see her.

The above illustrates part of a Chinese calendar.

1 月 yīyuè or **一月** yīyuè means "January."

2 月 èr yuè or **二月** èr yuè means "Feburary."

3 月 sān yuè or **三月** sān yuè means "March."

10 月 shí yuè or **十月** shí yuè means "October."

11 月 shí yīyuè or **十一月** shí yīyuè means "November."

12 月 shí èr yuè or **十二月** shí èr yuè means "December."

1 月 2 日 yīyuè èr rì or **一月二日** yīyuè èr rì means "January 2."

2 月 1 日 èr yuè yīrì or **二月一日** èr yuè yīrì means "Feburary 1."

2 月 2 日 èr yuè èr rì or **二月二日** èr yuè èr rì means "Feburary 2."

2 月 3 日 èr yuè sān rì or **二月三日** èr yuè sān rì means "Feburary 3."

黑白 hēi bái can be used to describe "black and white" or "right and wrong."

十二时正(十二時正) shí èr shí zhèng means "12 o'clock sharp."

日日是好日！rì rì shì hǎo rì means "Every day is a good day."

日又一日走了三个月，他看到了白熊！
(日又一日走了三個月，他看到了白熊！)
rì yòu yī rì zǒu le sān gè yuè   tā kàn dào le bái xióng
He saw the white bear, after he walked everyday for 3 months.

我只是看门的人。(我只是看門的人。)
wǒ zhǐ shì kàn mén de rén
I am only the person who guards the entrance.

我只是看门人。(我只是看門人。)
tā men shì yī lù rén   I am only the gatekeeper.

他们是一路人！(他們是一路人！)
tā men shì yī lù rén
They are the same group of gang members or people.

妳看到的是后门。(妳看到的是後門。)
nǎi kàn dào de shì hòu mén
The door you saw is the back door.

他有门人吗？你是他的门人吗？
(他有門人嗎？你是他的門人嗎？)
tā yǒu mén rén ma   nǐ shì tā de mén rén ma
Does he have disciples? Are you his disciple?

他私心太重！tā sī xīn tài zhòng means "He has too many selfish considerations."

快！到你了！kuài dào nǐle means "Quick! It's your turn!"

是吗？到我了吗？(是嗎？到我了嗎？) shì ma dào wǒ le ma means "Really? Is it my turn?"

我白说了！(我白說了！) wǒ bái shuō le means "My words were wasted!"

女装(女裝) nǚ zhuāng means "women's clothing."

你有子女吗？(你有子女嗎？)
nǐ yǒu zǐ nǚ ma   Do you have children?
子女 zǐ nǚ means "children."

你看到一个女子吗？(你看到一個女子嗎？) nǐ kàn dào yī gè nǚ zǐ ma means "Did you see a woman?"
女子 zǐ nǚ means "woman."

他来自中国。(他來自中國。)
tā lái zì zhōng guó   He is from China.

他来自中国吗？(他來自中國嗎？)
tā lái zì zhōng guó ma   Is he from China?

他太自不量力！tā tài zì bú liàng lì
He overestimates his own ability.

他在风口吹风。(他在風口吹風。)
tā zài fēng kǒu chuī fēng
He enjoys the wind by standing in the draft.

风口（風口）fēng kǒu means "draft."

口服 kǒu fú means "to take (medicine) orally."

人口 rén kǒu often means "population."

大衣 dà yī means "overcoat."

三心二意 sān xīn èr yì means "half-hearted."

木耳 mù ěr means "edible tree fungus."

白木耳 bái mù ěr is edible/gelatinous white tree fungus.

黑木耳 hēi mù ěr is edible/gelatinous black tree fungus.

他是个土人！（他是個土人！）tā shì gè tǔ rén
means "he is an aboriginal person."

土山 tǔ shān means "hill without rocks."

他看来好土！（他看來好土！）
tā kàn lái hǎo tǔ   He dresses like a country bumpkin.

他不到二十。tā bú dào èr shí means "He is under
twenty." 他不到三十。tā bú dào sān shí means "He is
under thirty."

他能一目十行。tā néng yī mù shí háng (literally "He
can read ten lines at one glance") means "He can read very
fast."

他一目十行，你能一目十行吗？
（他一目十行，你能一目十行嗎？）
tā yī mù shí háng   nǐ néng yī mù shí háng ma
He can read very fast. Can you read very fast?

他看到熊时，逃不了了，只好立刻倒下装死。
(他看到熊時，逃不了了，只好立刻倒下裝死。)
tā kàn dào xióng shí   táo bù liǎo le   zhǐ hǎo lì kè dǎo
xià zhuāng sǐ
When he saw the bear, it was too late to run away, so he had to
immediately fall over down upon the ground to play dead.

他说的不好，你说说看！
(他說的不好，你說說看！)
tā shuō de bù hǎo   nǐ shuō shuō kàn
He didn't present it very well. Would you like to try?

你在说什么？(你在說什麼？)
nǐ zài shuō shí me   What are you talking about?

他是个心中有什么就说什么的人！
(他是個心中有什麼就說什麼的人！)
tā shì gè xīn zhōng yǒu shí me jiù shuō shí me de rén
He says everything on his mind.

你为什么不来？(你為什麼不來？)
nǐ wèi shí me bù lái   Why didn't you come?

你我不是外人！
nǐ wǒ bú shì wài rén   We are friends!
(This is one way to say: We are friends!)
外人 wài rén means "outsider."

他是个中国人，不是外国人！
(他是個中國人，不是外國人！)
tā shì gè zhōng guó rén   bú shì wài guó rén
He is a Chinese. He is not a foreigner.

他问你好！（他問你好！）
tā wèn nǐ hǎo   He sends you his greetings.

大麻 dà má means "marijuana."

竹林后面，是什么？（竹林後面，是什麼？）
zhú lín hòu miàn   shì shí me
What's at back of the bamboo grove?
竹林 zhú lín means "bamboo grove."

竹林后面，你看到什么？
（竹林後面，你看到什麼？）
zhú lín hòu miàn   nǐ kàn dào shí me
What did you see at back of the bamboo grove?

竹林后面，你能看到什么？
（竹林後面，你能看到什麼？）
zhú lín hòu miàn   nǐ néng kàn dào shí me
What could you see at back of the bamboo grove?

看到大熊的是谁？（看到大熊的是誰？）
kàn dào dà xióng de shì shuí
Who is the person who saw the bear?

说你的是他人！（說你的是他人！）
shuō nǐ de shì tā rén
It's another person who criticized you!

说你的是他！（說你的是他！）
shuō nǐ de shì tā   It's him who criticized you!

这是个死火山！（這是個死火山！）

zhè shì gè sǐ huǒ shān   This is a dead volcano!

这是个死火山吗？(這是個死火山嗎？)
zhè shì gè sǐ huǒ shān ma   Is this a dead volcano!?

这不是个死火山吗？(這不是個死火山嗎？)
zhè bú shì gè sǐ huǒ shān ma   Isn't this a dead volcano?

外面在下大雨吗？(外面在下大雨嗎？)
wài miàn zài xià dà yǔ ma   Is it raining hard outside?

外面是不是下雨了？
wài miàn shì bú shì xià yǔ le   Is it raining outside?

他是个大力士。(他是個大力士。)
tā shì gè dà lì shì   He is a person of great strength.

水鸟(水鳥) shuǐ niǎo means "waterfowl."
中耳 zhōng ěr means "the middle ear."
快门(快門) kuài mén means "shutter (of a camera)."

这是你的日记吗？(這是你的日記嗎？)
zhè shì nǐ de rì jì ma   Is this your diary?
日记(日記) rì jì means "diary."

这是什么人的日记？
(這是什麼人的日記？)
zhè shì shí me rén de rì jì   Whose diary is this?

我的日记。(我的日記。) wǒ de rì jì means "my diary."

We have leraned some simple Chinese characters. The following shows some Chinese characters seen in Chinese tradional makets or streets.

你看到门口大树上的大鸟吗？
(你看到門口大樹上的大鳥嗎？)

nǐ kàn dào mén kǒu dà shù shàng de dà niǎo ma
Did you see the big birds on the big tree in front of the house?

门口(門口) mén kǒu means "doorway."

这人是大好人！(這人是大好人！)

zhè rén shì dà hǎo rén
This person is such a good man.
(This person is one in a million.)

The above handwritten characters are slightly different from the printed characters. It shows Chinese characters can be written quite creatively, as long as people can recognize them. (If you like, you can write Chinese characters your own style.)

大水一来，他就逃走了！
(大水一來，他就逃走了！)

dà shuǐ yī lái　tā jiù táo zǒu le
As soon as the flood came, he fled away.

这衣服很好看！
(這衣服很好看！)

zhè yī fú hěn hǎo kàn　　The clothes are very good-looking.

烈日下，三个行人走在路上。

(烈日下，三個行人走在路上。)

liè rì xià   sān gè háng rén zǒu zài lù shàng

3 people were walking under scorching sun.

他是个水手，我不是水手。

(他是個水手，我不是水手。)

tā shì gè shuǐ shǒu   wǒ bú shì shuǐ shǒu

He is a sailor but I am not a sailor.

水手 shuǐ shǒu means "sailor."

(We can see that Chinese people's handwriting is so different.)

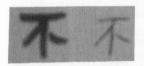

我能用...吗？(我能用...嗎？)

我能用这把刀吗？不行！

(我能用這把刀嗎？不行！)

wǒ néng yòng zhè bǎ dāo ma   bù xíng

May I use this knife? No!

我能用这把刀吗？行！(我能用這把刀嗎？行！)

wǒ néng yòng zhè bǎ dāo ma   xíng

May I use this knife? Ok!

Yes, We Can!

是的, 我们能!

是的, 我們能!

	yes		we		can
	是的		我们（我們）		能
Page	65	33	36	40	8

Yes, You Can!

是的, 你能!

	yes		you	can
	是的		你	能
Page	65	33	38	8

Yes, I Can!

是的, 我能!

Pronunciation
Reference
Chinese-Pinyin-MPS

Enjoy a break.
Tell the author!

samsong. author@msa. hinet. net

* how you feel while reading the book

* your favorite / least favorite part

* your learning experiences and explain why
  you chose to read this book

* what you like/disliked about author's writing
  style

* what worked and what needs work

* **Would you suggest a topic?**

Your book review or letter will inspire the
author to keep writing excellent books for
readers!

Pronunciation Reference

(TC: Traditional Chinese   SC: Simplified Chinese   MPS: Mandarin Phonetic System)

Page	TC	SC	Pinyin	Tone	MPS
83	風	风	fēng	1	ㄈㄥ
83	虫	蟲	chóng	2	ㄔㄨㄥˊ
84	與	与	yǔ	3	ㄩˇ
85	大		dà	4	ㄉㄚˋ
85	太		tài	4	ㄊㄞˋ
85	陽	阳	yáng	2	一ㄤˊ
88	正		zhèng	4	ㄓㄥˋ
89	在		zài	4	ㄗㄞˋ
91	爭	争	zhēng	1	ㄓㄥ
92	論	论	lùn	4	ㄌㄨㄣˋ
92	言		yán	2	一ㄢˊ
94	力		lì	4	ㄌ一ˋ
94	量		liàng	4	ㄌ一ㄤˋ
96	誰	谁	shéi	2	ㄕㄟˊ
97	的		de	5	ㄉㄜ˙
99	這	这	zhè	4	ㄓㄜˋ
101	時	时	shí	2	ㄕˊ
101	寺		sì	4	ㄙˋ

Pronunciation Reference

Page	Chinese	Pinyin	Tone	MPS
				(MPS: Mandarin Phonetic System)
101	寸	cùn	4	ㄘㄨㄣˋ
104	行	xíng	2	ㄒㄧㄥˊ
106	介	jiè	4	ㄐㄧㄝˋ
106	固	gù	4	ㄍㄨˋ
106	個　个	gè	4	ㄍㄜˋ
109	走	zǒu	3	ㄗㄡˇ
110	路	lù	4	ㄌㄨˋ
111	上	shàng	4	ㄕㄤˋ
111	下	xià	4	ㄒㄧㄚˋ
112	說　说	shuō	1	ㄕㄨㄛ
113	能	néng	2	ㄋㄥˊ
114	使	shǐ	3	ㄕˇ
114	史	shǐ	3	ㄕˇ
114	吏	lì	4	ㄌㄧˋ
116	脫	tuō	1	ㄊㄨㄛ
117	衣	yī	1	ㄧ
117	服	fú	4	ㄈㄨˊ
119	就	jiù	4	ㄐㄧㄡˋ
121	藏	cáng, zàng	2,4	ㄘㄤˊ, ㄗㄤˋ

Pronunciation Reference

(TC: Traditional Chinese   SC: Simplified Chinese   MPS: Mandarin Phonetic System)

Page	TC	SC	Pinyin	Tone	MPS
123	鳥	鸟	niǎo	3	ㄋㄧㄠˇ
123	烏	乌	wū	1	ㄨ
123	火		huǒ	3	ㄏㄨㄛˇ
123	黑		hēi	1	ㄏㄟ
125	雲	云	yún	2	ㄩㄣˊ
125	雨		yǔ	3	ㄩˇ
127	後	后	hòu	4	ㄏㄡˋ
127	面		miàn	4	ㄇㄧㄢˋ
131	開	开	kāi	1	ㄎㄞ
131	始		shǐ	3	ㄕˇ
131	口		kǒu	3	ㄎㄡˇ
135	出		chū	1	ㄔㄨ
136	吹		chuī	1	ㄔㄨㄟ
137	刮		guā	1	ㄍㄨㄚ
137	舌		shé	2	ㄕㄜˊ
139	越		yuè	4	ㄩㄝˋ
141	猛		měng	3	ㄇㄥˇ
141	孟		mèng	4	ㄇㄥˋ

Pronunciation Reference

Page	Chinese	Pinyin	Tone	MPS
				(MPS: Mandarin Phonetic System)
141	烈	liè	4	ㄌㄧㄝˋ
141	列	liè	4	ㄌㄧㄝˋ
144	是	shì	4	ㄕˋ
146	爪	zhuǎ	3	ㄓㄨㄚˇ
146	抓	zhuā	1	ㄓㄨㄚ
147	緊 紧	jǐn	3	ㄐㄧㄣˇ
149	自	zì	4	ㄗˋ
149	己	jǐ	3	ㄐㄧˇ
153	來 来	lái	2	ㄌㄞˊ
154	弓	gōng	1	ㄍㄨㄥ
154	了	le	5	ㄌㄜ˙
155	暖	nuǎn	3	ㄋㄨㄢˇ
157	照	zhào	4	ㄓㄠˋ
158	向	xiàng	4	ㄒㄧㄤˋ
160	熱 热	rè	4	ㄖㄜˋ
162	很	hěn	3	ㄏㄣˇ
163	快	kuài	4	ㄎㄨㄞˋ
164	把	bǎ, bà	3,4	ㄅㄚˇ, ㄅㄚˋ
167	外	wài	4	ㄨㄞˋ

Pronunciation Reference

(TC: Traditional Chinese   SC: Simplified Chinese   MPS: Mandarin Phonetic System)

Page	TC	SC	Pinyin	Tone	MPS
167	夕		xī	1	ㄒㄧ
169	寓		yù	4	ㄩˋ
169	意		yì	4	ㄧˋ
169	音		yīn	1	ㄧㄣ
172	溫		wēn	1	ㄨㄣ
174	和		hé	2	ㄏㄜˊ
175	巾		jīn	1	ㄐㄧㄣ
175	常		cháng	2	ㄔㄤˊ
177	更		gèng	4	ㄍㄥˋ
180	為	为	wéi, wèi	2,4	ㄨㄟˊ, ㄨㄟˋ
183	有		yǒu	3	ㄧㄡˇ
185	交		jiāo	1	ㄐㄧㄠ
185	效		xiào	4	ㄒㄧㄠˋ

[